W9-AZD-216

UNITED STATES CAPITOL HISTORICAL SOCIETY

Chartered in Washington, D.C., in accordance with the laws of the United States as a nonprofit, educational organization for publicizing and preserving the history and tradition of the United States Capitol. In addition to this book, the Society publishes the *Capitol Dome*, a quarterly newsletter; *We, the People*, a historical calendar; and for children, *A Young Person's Guide to the U. S. Capitol* and *Exploring Capitol Hill*. Active membership in the Society is open to all residents of the United States. Address inquiries to the United States Capitol Historical Society, 200 Maryland Avenue, N. E., Washington, D. C. 20002.

OFFICERS

Hon. Ronald A. Sarasin, *President*; Neale Cosby, *Treasurer*; Suzanne Dicks, *General Secretary*; Rebecca Evans, Donald R. Kennon, Paul McGuire, Diana Wailes, *Vice Presidents*; Dennis Molloy, *Legal Counsel*

EXECUTIVE COMMITTEE

Tamra Bentsen, Donald Carlson, Hon. E. Thomas Coleman, Neale Cosby, Suzanne Dicks, Frederick Graefe, Bryce Larry Harlow, Bruce Heiman, Hon. James Longley, Jr., Tim Lynch, David Regan, Hon. Ronald A. Sarasin

BOARD OF TRUSTEES

Hon. E. Thomas Coleman, *Chairman*; Ethel Schwengel, *Chair, Emeritus Board*; Gary Abrecht, Dr. Richard Baker, Tamra Bentsen, Senator Richard Burr, Don Carlson, Neale Cosby, Suzanne Dicks, Gloria Story Dittus, Nancy Dorn, James Dyer, David Geanacopoulos, Frederick Graefe, Senator Tom Harkin, Bryce Larry Harlow, Leslie Hayes, Bruce Heiman, Mark Hopkins, Charles Johnson, Bruce Josten, Hon. James Longley, Jr., Tim Lynch, Hon. Norm Mineta, Linda Monk, Anne Neal, Marty Paone, Beverly Perry, Hon. David Price, David Regan, Cookie Roberts, Mike Ruehling, Hon. Ronald A. Sarasin, Robert Schwengel, M.D., Dontai Smalls, Tina Tate, Hon. Pat Tiberi, Stewart Van Scoyoc, Hon. Zach Wamp, Debbie White, Candida Wolff

HISTORY DEPARTMENT

Donald R. Kennon, Ph.D., *Chief Historian*; Lauren Borchard, *Associate Historian*

First Edition produced by the National Geographic Society as a public service: Lonnelle Aikman, *Author;* Jules B. Billard, *Editorial Director;* Robert L. Breeden, *Design and Production Director;* George F. Mobley, *Photography*

Staff for the Sixteenth Edition: Diana E. Wailes, *Design and Production Coordinator;* Randy Groves, *Photography and Editorial Coordinator*

Special thanks for the assistance in the preparation of this edition to the staffs of the Architect of the Capitol, the Curator of the Architect of the Capitol, the Historic Preservation Officer, the Capitol Visitor Center, the United States Capitol Police, the Office of Art and Archives and the Office of the Historian of the United States House of Representatives, the Office of Photography of the United States House of Representatives, the Office of Speaker of the United States House of Representatives, the U.S. Senate Committee on Rules and Administration, the Senate Photographic Studio, the Office of Curator of the United States Senate, and the Office of the Historian of the United States Senate.

Copyright © 1963, 1964, 1965, 1966, 1967, 1969, 1970 1972, 1973, 1974, 1976, 1978, 1981, 1985, 1991, 2002, 2011, UNITED STATES CAPITOL HISTORICAL SOCIETY

Sixteenth Edition
Library of Congress Control Number: 2010939758
ISBN # 978-0-9831087-0-2

ARCHITECT OF THE CAPITOL

STATUE OF FREEDOM

The 19½-foot, 7½-ton bronze figure reigns atop the Capitol dome (preceding pages). Sculptor Thomas Crawford planned Freedom's headdress to be the soft cap of freed Roman slaves. He substituted a helmet with eagle head and feathers to meet the objections of then Secretary of War Jefferson Davis.

Foreword

In the foreword to the first edition of *We, the People* in 1963, Congressman Fred Schwengel, the founding president of the United States Capitol Historical Society, quoted 19th-century jurist Rufus Choate, who observed: "We have built no national temples but the Capitol. We consult no common oracle but the Constitution." This book was designed to tell the story of the past and promise of the temple of American government.

Since its first publication in 1963, *We, the People* has stood the test of time as a guidebook to the history and meaning of the United States Capitol. This sixteenth edition is the book's first major revision, made necessary by the recent completion of the Capitol Visitor Center. Readers will find in these pages the story of how the Capitol came to be, how it grew, and why it still stands today as a symbol in stone of the nation's experiment in representative self-government.

The success of *We, the People* would have been impossible without the support of the National Geographic Society and Melville Bell Grosvenor, its then president and editor in the creation of the book's original edition.

The late Dr. Melvin M. Payne, former chairman emeritus of the National Geographic Society and former vice president and trustee of the U.S. Capitol Historical Society, secured the funds and talent to produce that first edition.

Robert L. Breeden, former senior vice president of the National Geographic Society and a former trustee and chairman of the board of the U.S. Capitol Historical Society, has piloted *We, the People* through its many editions. The late Lonnelle Aikman, wrote the book's original text.

The production of all sixteen editions benefited from the assistance of the Office of Architect of the Capitol, currently headed by Stephen T. Ayers, and formerly by architects George M. White and Alan M. Hantman. Most of all, the cooperation of the United States Congress, its members, officers, and staff have made this book possible.

The U.S. Capitol Historical Society expresses its deepest gratitude to all of those who helped create this publication and who believed, as Fred Schwengel wrote in 1963, that "this book, like the Capitol itself, is for people everywhere who cherish freedom. Here is evidence of the struggles that have been made—and the struggles and sacrifices that must yet be made—to keep the ideals of equality of opportunity, of justice, and of freedom alive for all in the world."

Ronald A. Sarasin

President, U.S. Capitol Historical Society

MANUSCRIPT DIVISION, LIBRARY OF CONGRESS

GREAT SEAL *of the United States—an impression from the original die on a commission given George Washington, 1782.*

CONTENTS

INTRODUCTION

A Place

"IT IS NATURAL enough to suppose that the center and heart of America is the Capitol," wrote Nathaniel Hawthorne on a Washington visit in 1862, "and certainly, in its outward aspect, the world has not many statelier or more beautiful edifices."

The novelist saw the building almost complete, for the next year Crawford's Freedom was lifted atop the dome. He could not then assert what all would say now, that the Capitol is the best loved and most revered building in America. But he was right in stating that its combination of dignity, harmony, and utility made it a fit embodiment of the highest traits of the republic. Thornton's design, stamped with the approval of Washington and Jefferson, so happily expressed the majesty of our democracy that most of the state capitols reared since have echoed its lines. This, we may say, is the spirit of America in stone.

Doubtless everyone, gazing at the dome completed amid rigors of war, or entering the rotunda where Lincoln, Garfield, McKinley, Kennedy, and Unknown Soldiers have lain in state, thinks first of the august penumbra of history that enwraps the structure.

On its steps nearly all the presidents since Jackson have been inaugurated. The Capitol is where Lafayette was welcomed as symbol of one epochal alliance, and Winston Churchill as partner in another. In the Old House Chamber, now National Statuary Hall, every visitor must feel moved at the spot where John Quincy Adams sank under his mortal stroke in 1848. Who can enter the President's Room without reflecting, "Here it was that Lincoln

# of Resounding Deeds

indomitably defied his Senate leaders by refusing to sign the radical Wade-Davis bill upon Reconstruction." Some rooms are heavy with history. In the Old Senate Chamber, occupied from Buchanan's day by the Supreme Court, Webster replied to Hayne. The treaty closing the Mexican War was ratified. Clay and Calhoun battled over the Compromise of 1850. And later, many great Court decisions from the legal tender cases under Grant to the NIRA case under Roosevelt in 1935 were handed down.

Many of the transactions witnessed by Capitol walls still lift the hearts of men. Here Adams battled for the right of petition, and when one opponent offered a resolution for his censure as a traitor, he demanded that the clerk read the first paragraph of the Declaration of Independence as his answer. Here, as the House was trying Sam Houston for assaulting a fellow member, William Drayton of South Carolina declared that if freedom of discussion were ever restrained, the pillars of the Constitution would fall.

Here, in the middle of one war, Tom Corwin had the courage to proclaim that if he were a Mexican, he would welcome American invaders with bloody hands to hospitable graves; and just before our entry in another, Robert M. La Follette, Sr., halted the armed-ship bill amid a hurricane of denunciation. Here, when Andrew Johnson was placed on trial, a little knot of determined men vindicated the demands of justice and the authority of the presidency.

We can assert that the Capitol has heard eloquence equaling that of any parliament on earth; that it has written into law such immortal charters of idealism as the Fourteenth Amendment; and that in its foreign-aid bills it has enacted the most generous measures known to history. But our proudest boast is that no Capitol in the world has done more to safeguard free democratic debate, the privileges of minorities, and the fundamental civil liberties of man.

We would do an injustice to the spirit of the Capitol, however, if we emphasized merely the great men and dramatic events associated with it. The value of democratic government lies mainly in the place it gives to ordinary aspiring men and women. Since 1800 the Capitol has been the scene of grim, hard work by many thousands of conscientious legislators and their aides who have thought little of public fame, but much of the honest accomplishment of their tasks. We too often treat these servants, toiling early and late, as a matter of course.

If the stars were visible only once in a thousand years, wrote Ralph Waldo Emerson, we should await the spectacle with breathless interest; but our legislators, like the stars, are visible all the time, and hence are little noted unless of special magnitude. The Capitol is history; it is the major symbol of the nation, full of minor symbols; but above all it is a mighty engine, tended and kept throbbing by the indefatigable efforts of a select assemblage which represents far more of our national strengths than of our national weaknesses.

ALLAN NEVINS
(1890-1971)

On its hilltop, outlined sharply against the sky, stands the nation's Capitol, citadel of democracy

The Meaning of the Capitol

By LONNELLE AIKMAN

LIKE A VISION in fantasy, the great white dome of the United States Capitol rises above the trees at the end of converging avenues in Washington. Floodlit by night or cameo-cut against azure skies, it reminds Americans of classroom prints and pledges of allegiance, of high school Civics I, commemorative stamps—and a procession of domed and columned statehouses repeating the classic national profile all across the land. No other building, not even the White House, is so intimately linked with the lives of all the people of the United States. It stands at the heart of our system of representa-

epitomized in Alexander Hamilton's "Here, sir, the people govern."   CAROL M. HIGHSMITH, PHOTOGRAPHER

tive government. It is a focal point of American ideals of freedom and opportunity. It is proof—in stone, marble, and partisan debate—of the capacity of citizens to join in the adventures and satisfactions of governing themselves.

Here our elected representatives make the laws we live by under our Constitution, which begins, "We, the People of the United States, in Order to form a more perfect Union, establish Justice, insure domestic Tranquility, provide for the common defence, promote the general Welfare, and secure the Blessings of Liberty to ourselves and our Posterity, do ordain and establish this

Constitution for the United States of America." Here voices raised in legislative debate echo accents of 50 states. They speak of the conflicting interests of city, factory, and farm—of seaboard, plain, and the mountain regions in a far-flung nation. Then the votes are counted, and all voices merge into the majority that can speak as one for the United States.

There is a phrase for this democratic process. High atop the Capitol, it is incised on the base of the Statue of Freedom that crowns the dome. Taken from the Great Seal of the United States, it reads *"E Pluribus Unum"*—*"Out of Many,*

One," a phrase that captures the nation's purpose.

Such symbolism pervades the Capitol. It can be seen in structural and decorative details by dedicated architects and artists who labored on the Capitol. From pride in New World products, for instance, came the Indian corn and tobacco leaf designs chosen to ornament columns in the original Senate wing.

"This Capital [the column head with the corn-ear motif] . . . obtained me more applause from Members of Congress," architect B. Henry Latrobe wrote President Thomas Jefferson, "than all the Works of Magnitude, of difficulty & of splendor that surround them."

Paintings and murals displayed throughout the building highlight events of the founding, expansion, and development of the United States. Statues and portraits of the men and women who took part in these struggles and achievements—soldiers, statesmen, scholars, and inventors—line the marble corridors and look out from the columned walls.

T O THE THRONGS of sightseers who annually trudge the Capitol's immense distances, the whole effect is one of kaleidoscopic variety. Indeed, the panorama of so many ideas and objects might float off into abstractions or break up into fragments were it not that the exhibits, together, evoke the story of the United States as a nation.

It is this unifying element in our past that makes the home of Congress a tangible link between the states, recalling what Abraham Lincoln termed the "mystic chords of memory" shared by all Americans. In the Civil War, when critics complained of the cost of continuing construction, Lincoln himself cited the symbol of symbols.

"If people see the Capitol going on," a caller recalled him saying, "it is a sign we intend the Union shall go on."

All three branches of the government have had close associations with the Capitol since its first small wing was completed in 1800. For 134 years it sheltered the United States Supreme Court as well as the Congress. Here most of our presidents have been inaugurated, beginning with Thomas Jefferson, who in 1801 strolled over from his nearby boardinghouse to take the oath of office.

Highest-ranking officials of our three-way system come together in the House Chamber whenever the chief executive delivers the State of the Union address to a Joint Session of Congress, usually attended by the justices of the Supreme Court.

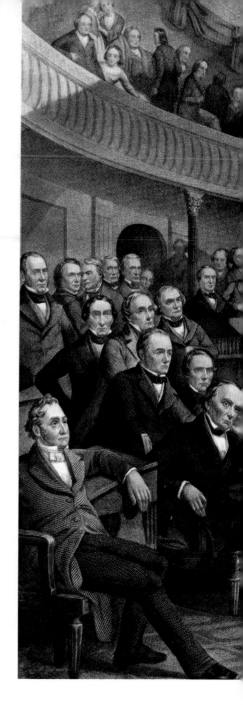

FATEFUL MOMENT *and dramatic action link nation and history within the Capitol's marbled halls. Here statesmen tread, strong wills clash, laws pass—today health care, in the past, a Compromise of 1850.*

10

ROBERT WHITECHURCH AFTER PETER F. ROTHERMEL

That event saw Henry Clay, aged and ill, plead to the Senate for a middle road in the North-South split over allowing slavery's spread to western lands. Daniel Webster (front row, second from left) listened, then put Union before self to speak for the compromise—and lost all chance at the presidency. Vice President Millard Fillmore presides here, his elbow above John C. Calhoun. William Seward, secretary of state under Lincoln, leans on the desk at right.

11

LINCOLN'S INAUGURAL in 1861 took place beneath hoists and scaffolds on the Capitol dome. Bayonets glinted as the president-elect spoke of possible civil war and reminded dissatisfied fellow countrymen of his oath to preserve, protect and defend the Constitution. Chief Justice Roger B. Taney then administered that oath in a scene (below) sketched by artist Thomas Nast.

Most presidents since Jackson have been sworn in on the Capitol's east or west fronts.

THE ILLUSTRATED NEWS, NEW YORK PUBLIC LIBRARY

More American leaders have dreamed, planned, worked, and argued in the Capitol than in any other single spot in the United States. Twenty-five of our presidents served in this building as representatives or senators, or both, before achieving the nation's highest elective office. Two of them, John Quincy Adams and Andrew Johnson, returned afterward to the House and Senate respectively.

"My election as President . . . was not half so gratifying to my inmost soul," Adams confided to his diary in 1830, after winning a seat in the Twenty-second Congress.

To Johnson, his welcome back to the Senate in 1875, after the humiliation of his impeachment trial as president in that same room, was even greater balm for wounded pride. In a chamber filled with rejoicing friends and disconcerted enemies, he received congratulations and flowers, magnanimously shaking hands with men who had voted for his conviction.

Some of the most dramatic events in our

FRANK LESLIE'S ILLUSTRATED, LIBRARY OF CONGRESS: P. HALL BAGLIE, WATERCOLORIST

political life took place at the Capitol, beginning with the vote by the House giving Jefferson the presidency over Aaron Burr after the electoral tie of February 1801.

During the first 60 years, Congress fought out the "great debates" over issues that split the country: foreign-trade restrictions and protective tariffs in the early 1800s; bank legislation of Andrew Jackson's time; slave- and free-state contests marking long shadows of the coming Civil War.

On a grieving April day in 1865, Lincoln's funeral cortege moved from the White House toward the Capitol that lately had flamed with gaslight celebration on Richmond's fall. In the rotunda, the body remained on view as thousands filed through the building to pay their last respects to the martyred president.

There, before a Joint Session of Congress, on April 2, 1917, Woodrow Wilson asked for a declaration of war against Germany. "The world," he said, "must be made safe for

13

democracy." And Franklin Delano Roosevelt, before a similar session, opened another presidential war message with the words, "Yesterday, December 7, 1941—a date which will live in infamy."

Soldiers, statesmen, poets—many others—have spoken here. On a February day in 1962, a modest, thoughtful man stood before Congress assembled to hear a report that would have seemed sheer lunacy not so long before. The speaker was Lt. Col. John H. Glenn, Jr.; the subject, his experience as the first American astronaut to whirl in space around the earth.

We have only begun," President John F. Kennedy told Congress in his January 1963 State of the Union address. "Upon our achievement of greater vitality and strength . . . hangs our fate and future in the world."

Ten months later an assassin's bullet had cut down America's youngest elected president. At the Capitol, his successor—former vice president and president of the Senate Lyndon B. Johnson—voiced a pledge:

"We will continue," Johnson said, ". . . that we may fulfill the destiny that history has set for us."

Along with crises and high moments, the Capitol witnessed the central miracle of a nation in the making.

In fact, action by Congress established all but a very few of the departments and agencies of the government; all owe their continued existence to the sanction of the people's representatives, whose far reaching and complex responsibilities today can be measured by the size and activities of the Capitol building itself.

In size—not including the recently added Capitol Visitor Center—the Capitol towers 288 feet, from east front base to the top of the Statue of Freedom. It is 350 feet wide and more than 751 feet long. Its floor area covers 16½ acres. Its 540 rooms hum with the sound and movement of committee hearings, administrative and maintenance work, and a thousand other operations devoted to the perennial consideration of legislation.

How this huge, labyrinthine building became the center and symbol of a nation that has existed for only slightly more than two centuries is an American success story all the more fascinating because it began in a wilderness and under the most unlikely circumstances.

ROTUNDA VISITORS *gather in the great circular hall beneath the Capitol dome. The cordoned passage provides an unobstructed walkway. The large oil paintings by John Trumbull depict scenes from the American Revolution: (from left) the presentation of the Declaration of Independence and the surrender of General John Burgoyne at Saratoga and of Lord Cornwallis at Yorktown.*

PENSIVE LINCOLN *dwarfs a tiny admirer. The work of Vinnie Ream (left), the statue stands at the west entrance of the rotunda. Ream was the first woman to receive a government commission for art.*

LIBRARY OF CONGRESS

A Building and a Nation Grow

NOT EVERYONE was pleased, in 1790, when Congress decided to establish the young republic's permanent seat on the banks of the Potomac River instead of accepting one of a dozen other sites offered.

"A howling, malarious, wilderness," some called the area chosen. "The Indian place . . . in the woods on the Potomac," said one disgusted official.

But the decision had been made, and much could be said for it. Washington, District of Columbia—marked off by, and named for, the first president—was near the midpoint of the long stretch of states. It lay close to the thriving centers of Georgetown and Alexandria, accessible to overland and water transport. "It is a beautiful spot, capable of any improvement," said Abigail Adams when she first saw her brief home as the wife of the second president, ". . . the more I view it the more I am delighted with it."

Few realized it then, but the embryo settlement also was favored by the vision of a city planner on the grand scale. Peter Charles L'Enfant, French-born engineer who had served under General Washington in the Revolution, laid out a city whose broad avenues and sweeping circles anticipated the needs of the future metropolis.

On a June morning in 1791, President Washington and L'Enfant made a horseback inspection of the landscape and terrain of the Federal District's site. L'Enfant had prepared a map and a report on the city's proposed features, including the home of Congress and the "presidential palace," linked by a broad green mall. "I could discover no one [situation]," L'Enfant wrote in his report, "so advantageously to greet the congressional building as is that on the west end of Jenkins heights." It stands,

PRESIDENT WASHINGTON, *wearing sash, collar, and apron of the Masonic order, lays the cornerstone for the Capitol on September 18, 1793. Dismantling in 1959 at the building's east front and tests in the 1990s failed to uncover the original stone. The marble-headed gavel and silver trowel Washington used still exist; they have figured in later stone-setting ceremonies at the Capitol and other public structures.*

1793

PAINTING BY ALLYN COX

17

MARYLAND HISTORICAL SOCIETY (BOTTOM) AND LIBRARY OF CONGRESS

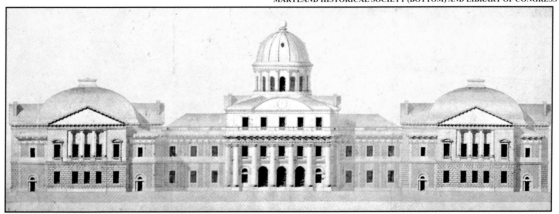

REDWOOD LIBRARY AND ATHENAEUM, NEWPORT, RI

LOW-DOMED BUILDING *won for Dr. William Thornton a 1792 competition for a Capitol design. His prize: $500 and a city lot. Washington praised the plan for its "Grandeur, Simplicity and Convenience." The original drawing was lost; this one dates back to the mid-1790s.*

CAPITOL DESIGN *by Stephen Hallet placed second in the contest. He was named to oversee construction on Thornton's draft, but, ambitious, sought to put in ideas from his own. Commissioners discharged him in 1794.*

OUTSIZE WEATHERCOCK *topped the Capitol building proposed by James Diamond, of Maryland. Other sketches submitted in the rivalry had equally impossible details or odd proportions; few trained architects then practiced in the United States.*

WILLIAM THORNTON—*physician, painter, and inventor—turned amateur architect to enter and win the competition to design the U. S. Capitol. Born in 1759 on a tiny island near Tortola in the West Indies, he had moved to the United States in the fall of 1786, after studying medicine in Edinburgh and living in Paris.*

The deadline for Capitol entries was just six days off when Thornton asked for and received permission to send his design in late. The plan that finally arrived "captivated the eyes and judgment of all," Secretary of State Thomas Jefferson noted in a letter to a colleague.

As one of three federal commissioners, Thornton clashed with Hallet and other experienced architects during the Capitol's construction. He became head of the Patent Office in 1802. A story credits his pleas to a British officer with saving that building from being burned in the War of 1812. Thornton died in 1828.

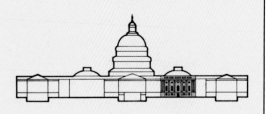

EAST FRONT

BOXLIKE WING *of the old Capitol, first to be completed, served Senate, House, and Supreme Court when this watercolor (top) was done in 1800. Small sketch shows the wing's location in today's building. Sandstone used in the construction came from Virginia quarries.*

he added in an oft-quoted phrase, "as a pedestal waiting for a monument."

To obtain a suitable design for their monument, the District of Columbia commissioners announced a Capitol competition, offering the winner $500 and a city lot. The contest was advertised in newspapers of the young country, but professional architects were few, and none of the entries proved satisfactory. Some were ludicrous—one design was crowned by a monstrous weathercock with wings spread wide.

At this crucial moment, a versatile young man named William Thornton (physician, portrait painter, steamboat experimenter, and amateur architect) gained permission to submit a belated design.

When his plan arrived, it "captivated the eyes and judgment of all," said another talented

amateur architect—Thomas Jefferson, then secretary of state.

"Grandeur, Simplicity and Convenience appear to be so well combined in this plan," George Washington wrote in a letter of recommendation to the District of Columbia commissioners, ". . . that I have no doubt of its meeting with . . . approbation from you."

By September 18, 1793, Dr. Thornton's design for a stately building with two wings joined by a domed center had been selected and modified. Troublesome construction problems had been resolved, and the time had come to lay the Capitol's cornerstone.

The day's program involved elaborate Masonic ceremonies, a common practice then, with roots going back to the link between medieval stonemasons and the order. As president, war hero, and Mason, George Washington had the lead role, supported by a uniformed and decorated cast from the Alexandria Volunteer Artillery and Masonic lodges of Maryland, Virginia, and the District. A parade began with the president's arrival on the Virginia shore of the

SLOOPS EDGE *Philadelphia wharves as the government moves to Washington from its last temporary capital in 1800.*

WILLIAM R. BIRCH, LIBRARY OF CONGRESS; JOSEPH E. BARRETT (BELOW)

"Grand River Patowmack," crossed to the Maryland side, and moved on to the President's Square, attracting more spectators at each meeting place.

"The procession marched two abreast," an observer reported in the September 25th issue of the *Alexandria Gazette*, "in the greatest solemn dignity, with music playing, drums beating, colours flying and spectators rejoicing."

Skirting the "great Serbonian Bog" that was then Pennsylvania Avenue, the marchers followed a new post road, broke ranks to step from stone to stone or teeter over a single log across Tiber Creek at the foot of Capitol Hill, and then proceeded to the hilltop building site.

There, Washington, wearing a Masonic apron reputed to be "the handiwork of Mrs. General Lafayette," conducted the ceremony with a marble-headed gavel and a silver trowel. He placed the cornerstone on a silver plate marking the date as the 13th year of American independence, the first year of his second term, and the year of Masonry 5793.

The plate's inscription praised Washington, "whose virtues in the civil administration of his country have been as conspicuous and beneficial, as his Military valor and prudence have been useful in establishing her liberties."

"The ceremony ended in prayer, Masonic chanting Honours, and a fifteen volley from the Artillery," the *Alexandria Gazette* informed its readership. "The whole company retired to an extensive booth, where an ox of 500 pounds' weight was barbequed, of which the company generally partook, with every abundance of other recreation." It was a brave beginning, but troubles were already brewing.

One of the difficulties was the rivalry

STONEMASONS *working on the Capitol chiseled personal trademarks on the stones they dressed. Most marks lie hidden in the construction or under plaster. These mason's marks show in a stairwell of the old House wing.*

JAMES HOBAN *gained a footnote in history by his prize-winning plans for the "President's Palace"—the White House—in 1792. But he also had a part in shaping the Capitol. Born in Ireland in 1758, he trained as an artisan and architect and immigrated to the United States after the Revolution. He lived in South Carolina and constructed plantation houses and public buildings in the Charleston area. Winning the White House contest brought Hoban an appointment to superintend construction. A year later the Capitol became his responsibility, too. He was Capitol superintendent until 1802, though his assistants Stephen Hallet and George Hadfield at times took rather free rein. Hoban was active in government building until his death in 1831.*

© 1958 JAMES HOBAN ALEXANDER

ARCHITECT OF THE CAPITOL

Claimed by Great Britain
and United States.

Claimed by Great Britain
and United States.

To Massachusetts

Area disputed
by Great Britain,
Spain and United States.

LOUISIANA

PURCHASE

SPANISH

VT

NEW YORK

N.H.

MASS

R.I.

CONN.

PENNA.

N.J

INDIANA
TERRITORY

OHIO

MD.

DEL.

KENTUCKY

VIRGINIA

TENNESSEE

N. CAROLINA

Ceded by
Georgia 1802.

GEORGIA

S. CAROLINA

MISSISSIPPI
TERRITORY

SPANISH

Area claimed
by United States
as part of purchase.

States

Territories

Unorganized, U.S.

Foreign

© U. S. CAPITOL HISTORICAL SOCIETY

LEWIS AND CLARK, *on funds voted by Congress, began their journey to the Pacific in 1804. The explorers are shown overlooking a Mandan village in the scene (top) from the Westward Expansion Corridor mural in the Capitol. The first official party to cross the Louisiana Purchase after its acquisition from the French, the expedition confirmed the immense value of the land. An unexpected bargain offered by Napoleon, the $15,000,000 purchase nearly doubled the nation's size. The Senate approved the treaty 24 to 7.*

ARCHITECT OF THE CAPITOL

BENJAMIN HENRY LATROBE
*took over construction of the
Capitol on his appointment as
surveyor of public buildings in
1803. An English architect, he
was born in 1764 and came to
the United States in 1796. Hiring
sculptors from abroad, he put
them to work executing ideas that
won acclaim, including corn and
tobacco motifs on columns (below).
Latrobe also had the task of
repairing the Capitol, burned by
the British in 1814, but resigned
in 1817. He died in 1820.*

between Dr. Thornton, the original designer, and a series of professional architects who wished to alter the prize-winning design.

Etienne Sulpice Hallet, or Stephen Hallet, as Americans referred to the French name, was the first to come to grief over this issue. Hallet's disappointment in having been rated second best in the original competition complicated the conflict. By the end of 1794, Hallet—in charge of construction at the Capitol—had been dismissed, and Thornton appointed to be one of the three District commissioners, who collectively had authority over the Capitol project.

MEANTIME, the sale of lots in the District of Columbia failed to finance the public buildings, as had been hoped. Commissioners hired a diverse workforce composed of white laborers and enslaved and free black workers. Skilled workmen, tools, and materials needed to build the Capitol proved hard to find.

Yet somehow work on the Congress House progressed. The first, or north, wing was completed under the general direction of the superintendent of construction, James Hoban, who designed and also directed the building of the "President's Palace"—the White House. Except for details, the wing was ready to receive the legislators by the autumn of 1800, when the government had moved, bag and baggage, from its last temporary seat at Philadelphia.

In the Senate Chamber on the ground level, under the intent gaze of spectators, President John Adams addressed the first Joint Session in the building on November 22, 1800. He wore the formal coat, knee breeches, and powdered hair of the time, and his words reflected the importance of the occasion. Not until Woodrow Wilson—on April 8, 1913—would another president appear in person to address the Congress.

"I congratulate the people of the United States on the assembling of Congress at the permanent seat of their government," President Adams said, "and I congratulate you, gentlemen, on the prospect of a residence not to be changed. . . . May this Territory be the residence

THE PAPERS OF BENJAMIN HENRY LATROBE, MARYLAND HISTORICAL SOCIETY

of virtue and happiness! In this city may that piety and virtue, that wisdom and magnanimity, that constancy and self-government, which adorned the great character whose name it bears, be forever held in veneration!"

Both the congratulations and the hopes must have echoed hollowly to the lawmakers as they prepared to settle down in the near-wilderness of the District of Columbia during that first winter of 1800.

"I do not perceive," Secretary of the Treasury Oliver Wolcott wrote his wife in Connecticut, "how the members of Congress can possibly secure lodgings, unless they will consent to live like Scholars in a college or Monks in a monastery, crowded ten or twenty in one house, and utterly secluded from Society."

The situation was hardly better at the Capitol itself, where the 32-member Senate and 106-man House, as well as the Supreme Court,

WEST FRONT

LATROBE'S 1810 MODIFICATION *(top) of the exterior in William Thornton's original plan joined House and Senate wings with a colonnaded central portico. The tinted section in the sketch depicts the House wing occupied in 1807.*

Circuit Court, and Library of Congress would soon share one modest rectangular building. Officials and clerks, however, could already see prospects for expansion in the partially laid foundations of the Capitol's central section and south wing protruding from the barren, stone-cluttered hilltop. And soon began a game of musical chairs, played by these august branches of government as they exchanged old quarters for new in a changing and growing building.

The House of Representatives moved first (1801), into a one-story, oval-shaped hall—appropriately nicknamed the "oven"—erected on the south-wing site. The oven was razed in 1804, and the members of the House of Representatives returned to their earlier quarters on the west side of the north wing. There they met for three more years while their own wing rose where the oven had stood.

The architect now in charge of the Capitol was Benjamin Henry Latrobe, appointed by President Jefferson in 1803.

As had Washington, Jefferson took a keen personal interest in the building's development, even to dictating many of its details. He particularly admired Latrobe's finished House Chamber,

SHOUTING HEADLINES in *Boston's* Columbian Centinel *of June 24, 1812, announce the step urged on Congress by fiery young "War Hawks" in its ranks. They called war "the only means of redress" for interference with American trade, impressment of American seamen, and other acts by Great Britain.*

with its carvings, classical columns, and visitors' gallery.

"I declared on many and all occasions," he wrote Latrobe, "that I considered you as the only person in the United States who could have executed the . . . Chamber."

Unfortunately, though all agreed that the new room was magnificent in appearance, its acoustics proved far from satisfactory. Virginia Rep. John Randolph of Roanoke summed up the verdict when he called it "handsome and fit for anything but the use intended."

While the House of Representatives hung red baize draperies behind Corinthian columns in an effort to muffle resounding echoes, the Senate grappled with its own brand of construction and moving-day problems.

Besides stopping leaks and patching cracks that threatened the north wing with premature decay, Latrobe rebuilt the east part of the wing, creating two rooms—one for the Senate and one for the Supreme Court a floor below.

During the renovation, displaced senators occupied quarters on the west side of the wing, then in January 1810 moved to their new chamber. In turn, the Supreme Court, then made up of

"THE BATTLE OF LAKE ERIE," *a painting by William H. Powell, hangs in the east stairway of the Senate wing. It depicts 28-year-old Oliver Hazard Perry transferring the colors from his battered flagship, the* Lawrence, *to the* Niagara *in the 1813 engagement.*

U. S. SENATE COLLECTION

BRITISH TROOPS, *ordered to "destroy and lay waste," set fire to public buildings in Washington on August 24, 1814. The act incensed Americans and shamed many Britons. "Cossacks spared Paris, but we spared not the Capitol of America," one newspaper said. This sketch appeared in London in 1815.*

REAR ADM. SIR GEORGE COCKBURN *took part in firing the Capitol. Reportedly, he stood on the House Speaker's chair and asked, "Shall this harbor of Yankee democracy be burned?"*

POPULAR HISTORY OF THE U. S., LIBRARY OF CONGRESS (TOP LEFT); GEORGE MUNGER, KIPLINGER COLLECTION

BURNED-OUT CAPITOL *stood stark after a rainstorm checked the flames. Piled furniture, books from the Library of Congress, and gunpowder made tinder for the blaze. Latrobe replaced the charred interior with marble, brick, and stone.*

A VOLUME OF TREASURY REPORTS *survived the fire. Handwriting on its flyleaf says Admiral Cockburn took it from the Capitol and gave it to his brother. A dealer presented it to the Library of Congress in 1940.*

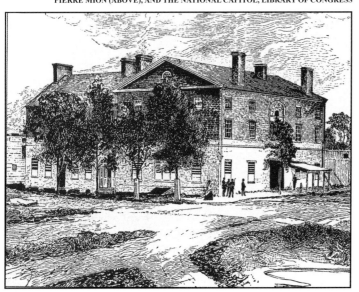

PIERRE MION (ABOVE), AND THE NATIONAL CAPITOL, LIBRARY OF CONGRESS

MONROE'S INAUGURAL

outdoors settled a dispute over whether to sit on the Senate's "fine red chairs" or the "plain democratic" ones of the House. His open-air oath-taking—later a tradition— occurred at the "Brick Capitol" (left). The building housed Congress during 1815–19 repairs to the burned quarters. A prison during the Civil War, it stood where the Supreme Court Building now stands.

seven members, transferred its sessions to the ground floor.

Presiding was Chief Justice John Marshall, whose brilliant career would build the Court's prestige as arbiter of the Constitution and lay a firm legal foundation for the legislative powers of Congress.

Hardly a dozen years had passed since the government's move to Washington, but already its leaders could look back with pride. They had built two wings of the Capitol and had made enough national history there to indicate that the building's scope was not excessive.

In 1803 Congress ratified Jefferson's vast Louisiana Purchase—though not without lively discussion as to whether it violated the Constitution. Congress voted funds for the Lewis and Clark Expedition, which revealed a new world of dazzling promise and sobering responsibility to men struggling in Washington to unify a string of independent-minded coastal states. And it appropriated money to strengthen the infant United States Navy for action against Barbary pirates preying on Mediterranean shipping.

Then came a day in November 1805 when a mission from the Bey of Tunis arrived in the village by the Potomac. The Senate received the Tunisian ambassador in its chamber, where that turbaned envoy expressed bewilderment at the spectacle of ordinary men being allowed to speak on the conduct of their government.

Less picturesque, but more significant, was the establishment by Congress in 1800 of a reference library. From the first $5,000 provided to stock the Capitol's one-room Library of Congress would come a world-renowned institution that now occupies three large buildings on Capitol Hill. The library now holds nearly 142 million items in collections of books, newspapers, periodicals, manuscripts, films, maps, and works of drama, music, and art.

"There is . . . no subject to which a Member of Congress may not have occasion to refer," Jefferson wrote in a wise observation still applicable today.

But first the young republic faced the War of 1812—and ordeal by fire—to determine whether either Capitol or, indeed, the nation itself, would have a future.

Congress declared war against Great Britain on June 18, 1812, after long and bitter debates between "War Hawks" and peace proponents over neutral rights, British impressment of American seamen, western lands, Indian affairs and other issues that created bad feeling between the two countries.

For many months after fighting began, most of the action took place far from Washington. Then, in the late summer of 1814, a British squadron under Rear Adm. Sir George Cockburn landed soldiers and marines near Benedict on Maryland's Patuxent shore. Brushing aside American forces hurriedly gathered at Bladensburg, the combined British force captured Washington on August 24 and set fire to most of its public buildings.

INDIGNANT PATRIOTS later claimed that Cockburn himself had led a detachment of troops into the House Chamber. They said he took over the Speaker's chair and put the rhetorical question, "Shall this harbor of Yankee democracy be burned?" The motion carried with a roar of "ayes."

The men ignited piles of flammable materials—chairs, desks, and books—in both House and Senate wings. The ensuing fires damaged interiors, scarred and blackened exterior walls, and destroyed the wooden walkway between the two wings.

Rain and violent winds swept through the city the following afternoon. The storm brought its own damage, destroying roofs, blowing cannons off their mounts, and killing American citizens and British soldiers.

Together with an accidental gunpowder explosion and a false rumor that American troops were gathering to retake Washington, the chain of disasters so shook British confidence that the redcoats moved out, never to return.

Amid the clamor of members demanding the government's transfer to another city, the homeless

Congress met that fall in the Patent Office Building, formerly Samuel Blodget, Jr.'s hotel—the only government office structure in the city to escape burning.

From late 1815 to 1819, congressional sessions were held in a new brick building hastily erected by a group of private citizens and rented cheaply to Congress as an inducement to stay on. This building, long known as the Brick Capitol, stood on the site of what is now the United States Supreme Court Building. There, on March 4, 1817, James Monroe took the presidential oath in Washington's first outdoor inaugural. The ceremony—"grand, animating and impressive"—was held outside, instead of in the House Chamber, to settle a deadlock on whether to use the House of Representatives' "plain democratic chairs" or transfer the "fine red chairs" from the Senate.

Meanwhile, the rebuilding of the Capitol proceeded under the direction of architect Latrobe, who had spent the war years away on projects ranging from designing Mississippi steamboats to planning waterworks for New Orleans.

On his recall in 1815, Latrobe found "the devastation . . . dreadful . . . a most magnificent ruin." Setting resolutely to work, he strengthened as well as restored both wings, using sandstone and marble, brick and stone. He enlarged and beautified the Senate Chamber, and redesigned the House Chamber into the semicircular shape we see today as National Statuary Hall.

CORCORAN GALLERY OF ART

SCARLET CURTAINS *in the Old Hall of the House hung as much for utility as for decoration—to muffle annoying echoes. Samuel F. B. Morse painted this night session of the House in 1822-23. Visitors now see the area as National Statuary Hall. Done before Morse turned from easel to telegraph experiments, the painting faithfully reproduced House details and members' likenesses. (Credit: Samuel F. B. Morse, The House of Representatives, 1822-23; oil on canvas, 86 1/2 x 130 3/4 in.; Corcoran Gallery of Art, Washington, D.C.).*

LAFAYETTE'S PORTRAIT,
*a gift to the U. S. by the artist,
Ary Scheffer, was presented to the
House of Representatives in 1824.*

COLLECTION OF THE U. S. HOUSE OF REPRESENTATIVES

But Latrobe, too, suffered from the occupational hazard of Capitol architects, disagreement with his boss, the commissioner of public buildings. After Latrobe resigned in 1817, he was followed in office by the able Boston architect Charles Bulfinch, the first American-born citizen to receive the appointment.

To Bulfinch goes the credit for completing the Capitol as Thornton and Latrobe had planned it. He worked out remaining decorative details of Senate and House chambers in time for Congress to move back on December 6, 1819. And Bulfinch carried through the building's long-planned central portion, including its east and west fronts, and a central rotunda covered by a low copper-sheathed dome.

"LIBERTY AND UNION, *now and forever, one and inseparable!" boomed Daniel Webster. His reply countered the states' rights stand of South Carolina's Sen. Robert Y. Hayne. The date: 1830. This painting of the Old Senate Chamber by G. P. A. Healy hangs in Boston's Faneuil Hall.*

NAMES CARVED *in a drawer of Webster's desk note other senators who have occupied the great orator's seat.*

34

CITY OF BOSTON

The cornerstone for the Capitol's center section was laid on August 24, 1818, four years to the day after the British conflagration. By October 1824, the rotunda interior was complete and ready for the city to hold a gala reception to honor a visiting dignitary and old friend—the Marquis de Lafayette. Fashionable Washington—eager to shake the hand of the French general and statesman who had helped create the nation—jammed the great circular hall.

In December, Congress officially received the Revolutionary War hero, making him the first foreign visitor to speak before a Joint Meeting. Lafayette was 67, but with charm undiminished by the years. To a remark made by Henry Clay, Speaker of the House, that he stood "in the midst of posterity," he replied that, on the contrary, he stood in the midst of his friends.

From the 1820s to the eve of the Civil War, the Capitol was the stage for momentous and tragic events—sometimes for scenes not far from comic opera. It was the era of leisurely oratory, filled with learned classical allusions, and on occasion with bitter insults that led

BUCOLIC WASHINGTON *in 1833 spreads around a domed Capitol and the White House. The flag marks the Washington Navy Yard. Traditionally, no nearby buildings may rise above the Capitol.*

STOKES COLLECTION, NEW YORK PUBLIC LIBRARY

WEST FRONT

BULFINCH'S DOME

and central addition gave the Capitol
this look from 1825 to 1856. City planner
L'Enfant called its hill site "a pedestal
waiting for a monument."

congressional opponents to uphold their honor on the dueling field.

It also was an age of chivalry, when gentlemen of the House and Senate welcomed visiting ladies to the floors of their respective halls, or, seeing their guests sitting for hours in hot and crowded galleries, would hand up refreshments of fruit fastened to the ends of long sticks.

But most of all it was a time of struggle and dissension, a period when sectional rivalries strained the bonds between the states and the national government.

The arena of test and decision was the United States Congress. Here opposing leaders wooed

KIPLINGER COLLECTION

FOGG MUSEUM

CHARLES BULFINCH *became the first American-born architect to have charge of construction at the Capitol. Boston-born in 1763, he received a Harvard education, followed by years of practical experience in building construction and wide study of architecture abroad. When Latrobe resigned in 1817, Bulfinch was appointed to succeed him on work at the Capitol.*

There the able Bostonian mainly carried out plans set down by predecessors, although he did modify Latrobe's design for the center building into the lines it has today. To him goes much of the credit for keeping construction of the Capitol moving toward completion.

Bulfinch left Washington in 1830, a year after his position as architect was abolished. Not until 1851 was there a successor—or need for one—except on a temporary basis. Bulfinch died in 1844.

followers and votes in verbal combats on such crucial subjects as internal improvements, the tariff, states' rights, and the conflicting interests of various sections of the country.

Within this same short time span, the Capitol also saw much to nourish America's increasing sense of national pride and "manifest destiny." In 1823, Congress heard the bold Monroe Doctrine proclaimed, warning Europe's rulers against intervention in this hemisphere. Congress voted for annexation of Texas in 1845, and the next year for war with Mexico and a treaty with Great Britain to settle the dispute over the far Northwest. By the end of 1848, these events had brought the Southwest, California, and the Oregon Territory under the United States flag. In January of that year, gold was discovered in California.

Now the sectional question hung heavy with threat. In the North-South battle to block or extend the spread of slavery to the West, which side would win? Or would both lose in the breakup of the Union?

For four decades the divisive rivalry called into play the talents and energies of some of the most dynamic men who ever sat in Congress. Three stood out as giants.

Spellbinder Henry Clay of Kentucky won his brightest laurels for his role in slavery-compromise bills of 1820 and 1850 that gave the South a temporary middle ground between secession and submission—and the North years of economic growth that made victory possible in the fratricidal war.

COLONNADED WALLS of the Old Senate Chamber once resounded to orations by John C. Calhoun, Henry Clay, and Daniel Webster. In lighter moments, gentlemen on the floor passed up refreshments by sticks to friends in the stuffy galleries.

In a mezzotint (below), the hall appears as it did in 1842. Engraver Thomas Doney made the print by peopling the gallery and chamber with individual daguerreotypes of senators and other noted persons. A present-day artist added color.

In 1976 the Old Senate Chamber was restored to look as it did when last occupied by the Senate in 1859 (right).

NEW YORK HISTORICAL SOCIETY; P. HALL BAGLIE, WATERCOLORIST (BELOW)

U. S. SENATE COMMISSION ON ART

ORIGINAL FURNISHINGS *of the restored chamber include the vice president's curved desk (upper dais) and Rembrandt Peale's portrait of Washington. Reproductions include the 64 desks and the curved gallery with its bronzed railing. The gilded eagle and shield (above), also original, was later modified and used above the bench of the Supreme Court, which occupied the room for 75 years.*

41

John C. Calhoun, of South Carolina, fought more often against Clay than with him, and ended his political career with a tragic plea for concessions from the North. Yet Calhoun's parliamentary genius, mastery of logic, and personal integrity earned for this champion of rights of a minority the respect of his colleagues.

Last of the three senators was Daniel Webster of Massachusetts. The most compelling orator America has produced, he poured his heart and thunderous eloquence into the struggle to preserve the Union. In his "Seventh of March" speech, he dramatically pleaded for Senate passage of Clay's 1850 compromise, but at high cost to himself. For daring to repudiate not only his Free-Soil followers, but also his own pledge to oppose extension of slavery—in any place, at any time—Webster was denounced by friends and lost his last chance of winning enough support to achieve what had been his greatest ambition, the presidency.

Throughout the long tumult, states continued to join the Union, population soared, and Congress grew. By 1850, the 62 senators and 233 representatives were beginning to feel crowded. Ironically, the drive for more space was spearheaded by Sen. Jefferson Davis, whose later fame as president of the Confederate States of America has overshadowed his earlier career.

Congress in September 1850 appropriated $100,000 to begin work on "ample accommodations for the two houses of Congress," an enlargement that would reduce the Capitol's original wings to the role of links between the additions and the central rotunda. President Millard Fillmore, authorized to select both the design and the architect, chose respected Philadelphia architect Thomas U. Walter to execute the design for the Capitol's extension.

The building's third cornerstone laying took place on July 4, 1851. It was an unqualified success, free "from all untoward occurrences," reported Washington's popular newspaper, the *National Intelligencer.* "The day was ushered in by salutes of artillery from different points of the city, and as the glorious sun gilded our tallest spires, and shed a lustre on the dome of the Capitol, it was welcomed by a display of National Flags and the ringing of bells from the various churches and engine houses."

President Fillmore and the grand master of the Masonic fraternity, B. B. French, each laid stones in elaborate civil and Masonic ceremonies. But the chief event for which the crowd had gathered from far and near was the dedication address by the old master, Daniel Webster, now secretary of state.

The most frequently quoted paragraph from Webster's two-hour speech was also part of his own handwritten statement that was placed beneath the cornerstone.

"If therefore," his deep, melodic voice rang out over the Capitol's stilled east plaza, "it shall be hereafter the will of God that this structure shall fall from its base, that its foundation be upturned, and this deposit brought to the eyes

MORSE'S TELEGRAPH *taps its historic message, "What hath God wrought!," on May 24, 1844, from the Capitol. The first long-range demonstration of the telegraph took place over wires between the Capitol and Baltimore, Maryland. Annie Ellsworth gives the inventor the message to be sent. Witnesses include Henry Clay, standing by Dolley Madison in the background.*

The Smithsonian Institution owns this key (right) used by Morse.

PAINTING BY PIERRE MION (LEFT)

of men, be it then known, that on this day, the Union of the United States stands firm, that their Constitution still exists unimpaired, and with all its original usefulness and glory."

Work on the massive additions to the Capitol went forward as fast as possible, but architect Walter faced many problems, including the usual conflicts over authority and a fire in 1851 that made it necessary to reconstruct the area housing the Library of Congress.

NEITHER WING was fully complete when House and Senate moved in—the House for its first session in the south wing, December 16, 1857, and the Senate in the north wing, January 4, 1859. The legislative halls, featuring arabesque decorations and intricate glass-and-iron ceilings, were illuminated by gas lighting at night. The House substituted upholstered settees for its desks in 1859, but only briefly.

Members voted to bring desks back the following year—and continued to use them until 1913.

Meanwhile, considering the precarious political situation of the 1850s, the Capitol's lavish furnishings and plans for the future seemed decidedly incongruous.

As the decade closed, the clash of wills in Congress reflected the country's rising tensions. Abolitionists and slavery diehards jammed the shiny new galleries, tossing out leaflets and hissing or cheering the impassioned speakers.

"Every man on the floor of both Houses is armed with a revolver," observed one senator. When a member accidentally dropped his weapon during a bitter eight-week struggle to elect the Speaker of the House, the uproar threatened to turn into mob violence. When secession came, and, one by one, the Southerners bade their colleagues goodbye, the scenes were

ARCHITECT OF THE CAPITOL

PIONEERS STRUGGLE *across a rugged divide in this mural at the west staircase of the House wing. Titled* Westward the Course of Empire Takes Its Way, *it was painted by Emanuel Leutze in 1862.*

Plains from Wyoming to New Mexico still show ruts cut by lurching wagons as waves of immigrants rolled west. They followed the lure of land and gold, and they peopled a burgeoning nation.

EXPLODING GROWTH *saw the nation fulfill a "manifest destiny" to stretch from sea to sea. Between 1840 and 1860, the population nearly doubled, to 31 million. The acquisition of land forced Congress to debate whether new states should be slave or free. The Compromise of 1850 quieted the issue for a time; the Kansas-Nebraska Act of 1854 rekindled sectional furies that led to war.*

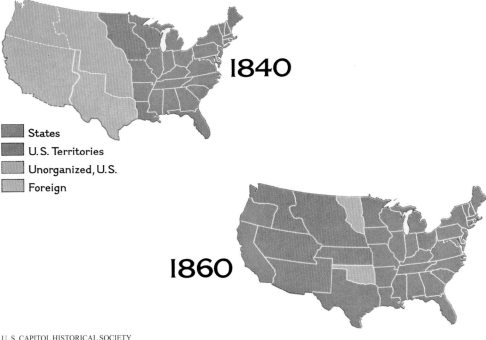

1840

- States
- U.S. Territories
- Unorganized, U.S.
- Foreign

1860

© U.S. CAPITOL HISTORICAL SOCIETY

HARPER'S WEEKLY (ABOVE AND TOP RIGHT), LIBRARY OF CONGRESS

SOLDIERS LOLL *in the rotunda in 1861. The Capitol served as barracks in the early months of the Civil War, then as a hospital for the wounded. Men called their quarters the "Big Tent." Here canvas shields rotunda paintings; a scaffold rises for construction of the dome.*

often stiff with dignity and poignant with pent-up emotion. No speech was more dramatic than the appeal to his colleagues, on January 10, 1861, by the senator from Mississippi—gaunt, courtly Jefferson Davis.

Like Calhoun, Davis pleaded for peace. He had tried to avert war, he told the senators and the presiding officer, Vice President Breckinridge of Kentucky, who also would soon be joining the Confederate side. "But if peace was not to be," said Davis, "then Mississippi's gallant sons will stand like a wall of fire around their State; and I go hence, not in hostility to you, but in love and allegiance to her."

In the gallery sat Davis's beautiful dark-haired wife, Varina. "We felt blood in the air," she would write later, "and mourned in secret over the severance of tender ties both of relationship and friendship; but a cloud covered all the rest, . . . we could even guess at the end."

THE SOLDIER IN OUR CIVIL WAR, COURTESY KATHERINE McCOOK KNOX

CAPITOL VAULTS *became storehouses for flour, beef, and pork when Washington feared siege at the war's onset. From stockpiles in arched passages, barrels skidded down planked steps to improvised bakeries. Ovens in basement committee rooms made bread for troops stationed at the forts and batteries ringing the city.*

HOISTED COLUMN

swings into place on the portico linking the old and new House wings. Two men at right have been identified as Jefferson Davis, a Mississippi senator when this 1860 photograph was made, and architect Thomas U. Walter.

CANVAS SHIELDS

men dressing columns. The House wing lacks porticoes finished in 1867 (right).

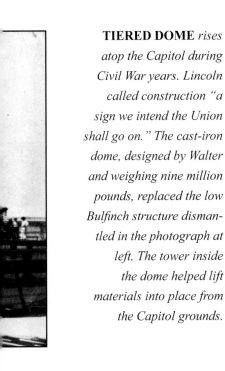

TIERED DOME *rises atop the Capitol during Civil War years. Lincoln called construction "a sign we intend the Union shall go on." The cast-iron dome, designed by Walter and weighing nine million pounds, replaced the low Bulfinch structure dismantled in the photograph at left. The tower inside the dome helped lift materials into place from the Capitol grounds.*

LIBRARY OF CONGRESS (RIGHT); (ALL OTHERS) ARCHITECT OF THE CAPITOL

CART-SLUNG COLUMN
of iron, one of 36 in the dome, arrives for placement. Maryland marble went into the Capitol extension's 100 exterior columns—each cut from a single block of stone.

49

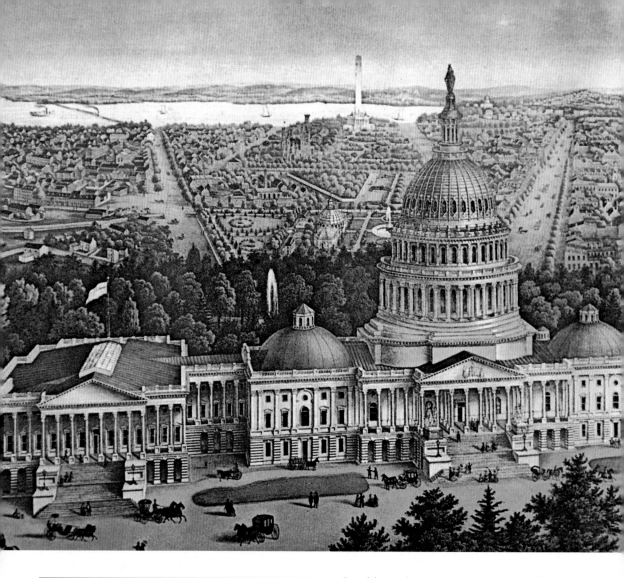

EAST FRONT

DOME AND WINGS *added to the Capitol in the 1850s and 1860s brought the structure to the form so familiar today. This 1871 lithograph (above), hand-colored, pictures it dominating a tree-dotted city. The Washington Monument, completed in 1884, is shown with a colonnaded base that was part of the original design but never built.*

Southbound congressmen were well on their way home when President-elect Abraham Lincoln arrived on February 23, early and unannounced, in the Washington railway station. The curtain was rising on the most fateful years the nation had yet faced.

At the Capitol on Inauguration Day, March 4, 1861, a tall, gangling figure stood on the wind-raked stand built over the east front steps. There had been rumors of a plot to blow up the platform. Riflemen watched from the windows behind the speaker. Below him glinted the fixed bayonets of a line of soldiers.

Adjusting his steel-rimmed spectacles, Lincoln looked out on a sea of faces, not all friendly, since Washington was filled with Southern sympathizers. To these people, and those in the South, Lincoln addressed his

KIPLINGER COLLECTION

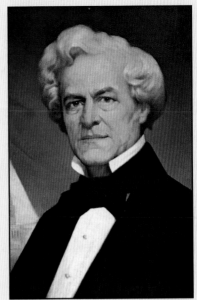

ARCHITECT OF THE CAPITOL

THOMAS USTICK WALTER
*guided construction during one of
the Capitol's most important peri-
ods of change. Named architect of
the Capitol extension by President
Fillmore in 1851, he served until
1865—eventful years that saw the
building grow threefold.*

*Walter's father and grandfather
were masons, and the Philadelphia-
born youth himself became a master bricklayer while also studying
in an architect's office. He set up
shop for himself in 1830. When a
contest for enlarging the Capitol
opened in 1850, Walter submitted
an entry.*

*Construction of the Capitol's
wings began immediately after
Walter's appointment. He ran into
many problems, including conflicts
over authority. The Capitol dome
he built is considered a notable
engineering feat.*

*Born in 1804, he died in 1887.
This detail of the portrait by
Francisco Pausas, based on a
Mathew Brady photograph,
shows him as Capitol architect.*

famous appeal for conciliation:

"In your hands, my dissatisfied fellow countrymen, and not in mine, is the momentous issue
of civil war. . . ."

"We are not enemies, but friends. We must not
be enemies. Though passion may have strained,
it must not break our bonds of affection."

But the firmness in Lincoln's inaugural
speech discouraged any hope that a compromise
with secession would be possible. "I hold," he
said, "that in contemplation of universal law,
and of the Constitution, the Union of these
States is perpetual. . . . no State, upon its own
mere motion, can lawfully get out of the Union.
The power confided to me, will be used to hold,
occupy, and possess the property, and places be-
longing to the government."

A month and eight days later, Confederate

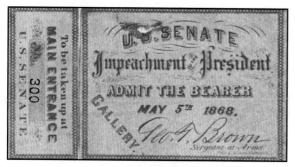

DICTRICT OF COLUMBIA PUBLIC LIBARY

THIS COVETED TICKET— *the Senate gallery had fewer than 800 seats—brought admission to the 1868 impeachment trial of President Andrew Johnson. Colors changed each day of the trial.*

CROWDED SENATE CHAMBER *hears Thaddeus Stevens read the House message of impeachment. Stevens led the attempt to punish Johnson for his opposition to Congress. Sitting as a court, the Senate failed by a single vote to convict. Had impeachment succeeded, the Constitution's system of checks and balances might have given way to a parliamentary type of government.*

PRESIDENT JOHNSON, *by his White House desk, accepts impeachment summons from the Senate sergeant at arms. As did Lincoln, Johnson favored leniency toward the South; he irked Congress by his stubbornness on Reconstruction and other administration issues.*

CARRIED IN A CHAIR, *Thaddeus Stevens enters the Capitol during the impeachment trial. Contemporary accounts called him "an infirm old man . . . upheld only by an iron will." He died a few months later.*

52

HARPER'S WEEKLY (LOWER LEFT) AND FRANK LESLIE'S ILLUSTRATED, LIBRARY OF CONGRESS

guns fired on Fort Sumter. For the rest of the war, the Capitol at Washington would be the Union's stronghold and symbol. The "Old Brick Capitol," across the way, would become a prison, housing for a while two famed Confederate spies, seductive Rose Greenhow and spirited Belle Boyd.

Congress was not in session when war broke out. Immediately the War Department took over the marble spaces of the newly enlarged Capitol as barracks for Northern regiments marching into the city on the president's call for 75,000 state militia. The men termed their quarters the "Big Tent," and boasted of portrait-hung parlors, comfortable sofas, and desks for writing

53

letters home. For a time 3,000 soldiers slept in the building, from the rotunda and legislative chambers to hall niches and airy nooks up near the unfinished, open dome. Mealtime found lines of hungry men waiting to cook rations of bacon, biscuits, and coffee at furnaces lighted in the basement.

The furnaces sparked an idea. Basement committee rooms were converted into a bakery that included large ovens lined with fire bricks. Flour was commandeered from the city's mills. The aroma of fresh-baked bread drifted about the Capitol as army bakers turned out enough loaves to feed soldiers in forts and batteries springing up around Washington.

By the next autumn the cheerful bustle and youthful high jinks of what had been romantically pictured as a short, gallant war had given way to harsher realities. The Capitol, like lesser buildings, became an emergency hospital. Set up in its historic halls, chambers, and rotunda were 1,500 cots, on which lay the sick and wounded streaming back from the battlefields of Second Manassas and Antietam.

Among the city's doctors—and a sprinkling of nurses stirred by the example of Dorothea Dix and America's future Red Cross founder, Clara Barton—moved a gentle, bearded man. Walt Whitman, poet and humanitarian, spent most of his spare time during the war in army hospitals, dispensing small gifts and large doses of cheer.

"The hurt and wounded I pacify with soothing hand," he would write later in a poem of remembrance. "I sit by the restless all the dark night, some are so young."

With the return of Congress, following the patients' transfer to other hospitals, the Capitol became the sounding board of fears and suspicions that fevered the air of the nerve-wracked city. Accusations rang out in legislative chambers. The Joint Committee on the Conduct of the War investigated charges of incompetence and conspiracy. Not even the president's home escaped the pointing finger. Gossips whispered that Mary Lincoln was a spy in the White House, seeking to protect relatives who were fighting on the side of the Confederates.

One morning at a secret session of investigating senators, the towering figure of Abraham Lincoln suddenly appeared before the committee table. One of those present recalled years later that Lincoln's eyes were filled with "an almost unhuman sadness."

The president told the astonished group that he had come of his own volition, "to say that I, of my own knowledge, know that it is untrue that any of my family holds treasonable communication with the enemy."

"By tacit consent, no word being spoken," the narrator reported, "the committee dropped all consideration of the rumors that the wife of the President was betraying the Union."

DESPITE FOUR YEARS OF WAR, the Capitol began to take on a new shape. Construction of a vastly enlarged dome—authorized by Congress in 1855 to replace the one dwarfed by the new wings—made the building even more imposing.

Designed by architect Walter, the big dome is a masterpiece of 19th-century engineering. Its outer and inner cast-iron shells are intricately girded and bolted together, weighing nearly nine million pounds of iron. Between the shells winds a narrow staircase of 183 steps.

To raise the heavy iron parts to their lofty places, construction superintendent Montgomery C. Meigs built a scaffold tower from the floor of the rotunda up through a temporary wooden roof. It served as a base for the hoisting devices used to lift the materials on the outside.

The great bronze goddess that crowns the dome's lantern structure was the work of an outstanding American sculptor, Thomas Crawford. He referred to her as "Freedom triumphant," and shaped her as a classical figure, with one hand on a sword, the other holding a wreath and resting on a shield.

Her feathered headdress has led many to believe that the statue represents Pocahontas or some other Indian. Actually, Crawford had

COLLECTION OF ROBERT A. TRUAX

OLD LIBRARY OF CONGRESS *quarters in the Capitol abound with ornate metalwork. As the library's collection outstripped shelf space, piles of books accumulated on the floor, as seen in this 1867 photograph. By 1890, bagged items leaned against columns of stacked books. The need for more space prompted a drive for the library's own building, finished in 1897. The library today is among the world's largest; its collection of nearly 142 million items echoes Jefferson's remark that "there . . . is no subject to which a Member of Congress may not have occasion to refer."*

COLLECTION OF THE U. S. HOUSE OF REPRESENTATIVES *(TOP AND BELOW LEFT)*

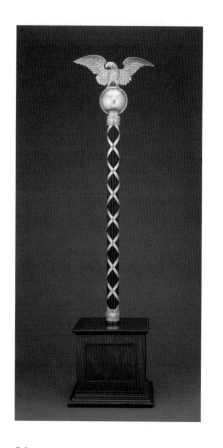

CARRYING THE MACE, *symbol of authority in the House, the sergeant at arms rounds up members for a quorum. This 1881 artist's conception appeared in* Frank Leslie's Illustrated Newspaper. *The Mace rests on a stand beside the rostrum except in rare cases when displayed before an unruly member to restore order. Its position at the rostrum tells whether the House is in "committee" or "session"— an aid for determining the number needed for a quorum.*

The first House Mace was destroyed when the British burned the Capitol. A painted wood facsimile substituted until 1841, when a silver-and-ebony version of the original was made (left). Its eagle and globe surmount rods representing the first 13 states.

OATH-TAKING CEREMONY *of Vice President Theodore Roosevelt, March 4, 1901, finds President-elect William McKinley (center) among the spectators.Until 1937 vice presidents took the oath in the Senate Chamber; later, they usually took the oath at the presidential inaugural ceremony.*

designed the headdress as a liberty cap, after those worn by Rome's emancipated slaves. He substituted a helmet with eagle head and Indian feathers to meet the objections of Jefferson Davis, future president of the Confederacy, who had charge of Capitol construction as secretary of war from 1853 to 1857.

Modeled in Crawford's Rome studio, the statue's plaster cast was imperiled by a leaky ship, heavy gales, and other hazards on an eight months' journey to the United States. By October 1862, the bronze form was cast at Clark Mills's foundry in Washington and the city's residents had an opportunity to inspect the 19½-foot figure temporarily displayed on the grounds of the Capitol.

Finally, at the appointed hour of 12 noon, December 2, 1863, the giant head of Freedom — last of the statue's five sections — was raised and bolted into place.

The United States flag, bearing 35 stars for all the states, Northern and Southern, fluttered overhead. Spectators cheered. Capitol Hill's field battery boomed a 35-gun salute, one for each state.

The interior of the Senate wing would be finished in the fall of 1864, but several more years would pass before its north and west porticoes were in place. By 1867 all the porticoes of the House of Representatives' wing also had been built, but it was 1916 before the sculptured east pediment for the House was at last unveiled.

Today, the Capitol includes two major additions—the Capitol Visitor Center *(see pp. 133–41)* and a 32½-foot eastward extension of the central area. This substantial enlargement won the support in 1955 of Sam Rayburn, member of the House for 48 years and its Speaker for 17, who steered bills containing the proposal past congressional hurdles.

PIERRE MION, AFTER AN ENGRAVING FROM HARPER'S WEEKLY

President Eisenhower laid the extension's cornerstone on July 4, 1959. A Masonic ceremony followed. Work went forward under the direction of the then Capitol architect, J. George Stewart. The new front was in place just in time for President John F. Kennedy's inauguration on January 20, 1961.

Nearly a century earlier Walter had called such construction "an architectural necessity" to balance the added wings and dome. Succeeding Capitol architects recommended the expansion against an outcry that no change should be made in America's treasured historic monument.

Pushing the building's midsection forward eliminated the impression that the huge dome overhung the central portico. The builders preserved, as interior supports, the walls that stood when General Lafayette visited the rotunda. At the same time they replaced the old sandstone front with one of durable marble, every detail of hand-carved decoration faithfully copied from the crumbling originals.

Sandblasters laboriously took 32 layers of paint from the ironwork of the dome. The replacement coats—requiring 1,750 gallons— were toned to match the marble of the wings.

INSIDE, the Capitol gained two and a half acres of space spread over five floors. Brought into being were 102 rooms, including individual offices, committee and reception rooms, dining rooms, kitchens, and entrance foyers.

There are additional elevators and—by no means the least of the useful innovations — private corridors that link the north and south wings. For the first time, members of the Congress could walk between Senate and House chambers and various offices without having to elbow their way through crowds of sightseers.

But would the Capitol ever be finished? For years opposing factions in the Senate and House debated the question of what to do about the deteriorating west front.

One group proposed that it be extended as was the east front to provide more space for offices and other facilities. The other group

wanted to repair and reinforce the crumbling sandstone walls of the west front built from 1793 to 1826, the only visible part of the original sandstone exterior.

A decision to repair and reinforce the west front was finally voted by Congress in July 1983; preservation and restoration began soon after. In the autumn of 1987, painting and other finishing touches concluded work on this historic and spectacular section of the Capitol.

Since 1908, six office buildings, three for the House and three for the Senate, have been built nearby to help fill the need for office

LIBRARY OF CONGRESS

space, committee hearings, and other activities of Congress.

The House structures were named for Speakers Joseph Cannon, Nicholas Longworth, and Sam Rayburn. The Senate trio honors senators Richard Russell, Everett Dirksen, and Philip Hart. The Hart Building alone added one million square feet of floor space.

The Rayburn Building, most recent of the House office structures, was completed in 1965. A massive edifice of marble and granite, it became the backdrop—in the spring and summer of 1974—for one of the great public dramas in

HUSHED JOINT SESSION *in February 1917 hears President Woodrow Wilson announce the severance of diplomatic relations with Germany. Four years earlier he had set a precedent by becoming the first chief executive to address Congress in person since John Adams did so in 1800. Beneath the flag, Vice President Thomas Marshall and Speaker James Beauchamp "Champ" Clark (in light suit) preside.*

59

HUGO H. HARPER

PRESIDENT COOLIDGE *bestows the Medal of Honor on Charles A. Lindbergh for his historic flight across the Atlantic.*

Often called the "Congressional" Medal of Honor, this highest of the nation's decorations is awarded by the president in the name of Congress for "gallantry and intrepidity at the risk of life." Others in the 1928 picture at the White House are Speaker Nicholas Longworth, Vice President Charles G. Dawes, and Secretary of War Dwight Davis.

LAUREL WREATH *and goddess Minerva embellish the Army's Medal of Honor. Reverse here bears Lindbergh citation. Navy and Air Force versions differ slightly in design.*

the history of American government.

The setting was Room 2141; the characters, 36 men and two women, members of the House Committee on the Judiciary. Their unrehearsed role was to weigh the evidence and debate and vote on articles of impeachment accusing President Nixon, under the Constitution, of "high crimes and misdemeanors."

The climax to the drama came near the end of July, with the final debates and votes televised live. As millions of viewers watched and listened throughout the United States, and by satellite abroad, the committee, with bipartisan support, overwhelmingly passed three articles of impeachment to be submitted for the consideration of the full House of Representatives.

If the House had approved the articles, as was predicted by many who followed the proceedings, the Senate would then have been required to conduct its second impeachment trial of a president of the United States. Instead, Mr. Nixon avoided the ordeal that Andrew Johnson had suffered 106 years before by resigning his office—

BLINDFOLDED *with cloth taken from a chair in Independence Hall, Secretary of War Henry L. Stimson begins the 1940 draft—first enacted by Congress in peacetime. President Roosevelt read the number Stimson drew, 158. The same bowl did duty in the 1917 wartime draft.*

HARRIS & EWING

UNITED PRESS INTERNATIONAL

61

the first chief executive in American history to do so.

Twenty-four years after Nixon resigned, another president, William Jefferson Clinton, faced trial by the Senate after impeachment by the House. Impeached December 19, 1998 on charges of perjury and obstruction of justice, Clinton was acquitted by the Senate on February 12, 1999.

The House Judiciary Committee thus became the most famous of such investigative bodies in modern times. But there are also hundreds of other committees and subcommittees of Congress that meet regularly on vital national and international issues in the offices and suites scattered throughout the Capitol and related office buildings.

In the light of the enormous amount and variety of business that Congress must now deal with, it seems strange to recall that no office space was provided for members of Congress prior to the purchase of an apartment building in 1891 for Senate offices. The first office building constructed was the House office building that opened in 1908.

E ACH NEW OFFICE BUILDING has brought an enlargement of the Capitol complex, now totaling more than 274 acres. The stately park around the Capitol itself holds an unusually fine collection of American and foreign trees—as well as a variety of shrubs and flowers. Cherry trees, dogwoods, azaleas, and tulips flourish here.

The Capitol's landscaping was carried out, starting in the mid-1870s, by Frederick Law Olmsted, designer of New York's Central Park. In those days, certain areas at the Capitol served for croquet games, and others for egg rolling by children at Easter. But perhaps the sharpest reminder of a vanished era appears in a routine report of 1877. Plants and bushes, it said, had been damaged by stray cows of the neighborhood.

Since such incidents, the Capitol has both reflected and affected the changes that have swept the country and the world. It has seen Congress grow to 100 senators and 435 representatives, plus the nonvoting resident commissioner from Puerto Rico and delegates of the Virgin Islands, Guam, American Samoa, Northern Mariana Islands, and the District of Columbia. So steadily did population expansion boost House membership that

GEORGE M. WHITE, *first professional architect selected since 1865, served as architect of the Capitol from 1971 to 1995. His credits included construction of the James Madison Memorial Building of the Library of Congress, the design and construction of the Philip A. Hart Senate Office Building, and restoration of the Old Supreme Court and Old Senate chambers in the Capitol.*

GLEAMING *in the autumn sun, the restored west front dwarfs visitors touring the Capitol grounds. When its central section—more than 160 years old—began to crack and crumble, one group in Congress favored extending the facade as a remedy. But preservation won out and set in motion work completed in 1987 to strengthen and preserve the old sandstone walls.*

Congress in 1911 limited the number to the presently voting 435.

The U.S. Congress belies the saying that those who make a nation's songs mold also its character. In laws passed here, a knowledgeable student can trace the entire course of modern America's economic, political, and social development.

Between the lines of Reconstruction legislation, one can feel the passions and furies of bitter adjustments. Thumbing through the homestead acts, the reader can almost hear the "whoop and holler" with which each wave of westbound pioneers took over the government's freely offered acres for cattle-raising, farming, and timberlands.

The rise of big industry and high finance, based on seemingly endless raw materials and subject to boom-and-bust speculation, brought regulation in such areas as interstate commerce, food, and drugs. In time came restrictions on investments, trusts, and monopolies, and laws to conserve the country's natural resources and to protect the environment.

In the arena of foreign affairs, President William McKinley's war message to Congress launched the Spanish-American War in 1898 and marked U.S. participation in world politics on an ever-increasing scale.

Twenty-first-century Americans can look back on legislation that has transformed the nation and their own

FLAG-DRAPED, *the casket of John F. Kennedy rests in the rotunda as dignitaries lead a nation's mourning for its murdered president. Congressmen, government officials, and other notable persons encircle the catafalque in the November 24, 1963, memorial services. Eleven presidents have been so honored in the rotunda. Presidents Abraham Lincoln, James Garfield, William McKinley, Warren Harding, and William Howard Taft preceded Kennedy; followed by Herbert Hoover, Dwight Eisenhower, Lyndon Johnson, Ronald Reagan, and most recently, Gerald Ford.*

GEORGE F. MOBLEY © N. G. S.

lives. Though we don't always realize it, our daily talk, newspapers, and TV often reflect changes brought about by congressional bills and the broad principles of constitutional amendments.

The process began with the Bill of Rights—the ten original amendments. The first and most familiar article guarantees freedom of religion, of speech, of the press, and the right of the people peaceably to assemble and to petition the government for a redress of grievances.

Other amendments adopted since 1791 include the right to vote (1870) regardless of "race, color, or previous condition of servitude"; the income-tax amendment of 1913; prohibition in 1919 (and its repeal in 1933); and woman suffrage in 1920.

Among still other life-touching legislation are social security, civil rights and medical-benefits bills, and currently, still-debated laws designed to cope with federal deficits versus social and military obligations.

All this, and more, has been built into the U.S. Capitol and is part of what visitors may see and sense in the home of Congress.

SENATE AND HOUSE meet in Joint Session on January 25, 2011, to hear President Barack Obama deliver his State of the Union address. The Constitution requires the chief executive to "give to the Congress Information of the State of the Union," The message traditionally is presented annually by the president in the House Chamber in the presence of the members of the House and Senate, the Supreme Court justices, cabinet members, and members of the Joint Chiefs of Staff.

Behind the president sit the vice president, Joseph Biden, and the Speaker of the House, John Boehner. Thomas Jefferson submitted his State of the Union addresses in writing rather than in person. Woodrow Wilson in 1913 reestablished the practice of delivering the speech in the House Chamber.

UNITED PRESS INTERNATIONAL

STATESMEN, AUTHORS, ASTRONAUTS — *all have addressed Congress: Winston Churchill after Pearl Harbor; Carl Sandburg honoring Lincoln; Frank Borman on behalf of American prisoners of war in Vietnam.*

ARCHITECT OF THE CAPITOL

Exploring Today's Capitol

STAND ON the Capitol plaza, facing the monumental east steps. There you occupy a spot from which Americans witnessed most presidential inaugurals since Andrew Jackson brought the ceremony outside to cheering followers in 1829.

Architect Bulfinch's central portico had just been completed. Spilling out from the plaza before it was a milling crowd of bankers, workmen, housewives, town merchants, and visiting frontiersmen, some of whom had walked far to see the triumph of the "People's President." Between the portico's towering columns and on its stone steps stood Washington's great men and their ladies. "Scarlet, purple, blue, yellow, white draperies and waving plumes of every kind and colour . . . had a fine effect," wrote a social commentator of the times.

On these steps during the Civil War, Lincoln spoke the compassionate words, "With malice toward none; with charity for all." There Franklin Roosevelt told a nation trying to lift itself out of the Great Depression that "the only thing we have to fear is fear itself." And John F. Kennedy said, "Ask not what your country can do for you — ask what you can do for your country."

Starting with Andrew Jackson, 27 elected presidents took the oath of office at the east front. On January 20, 1981, this precedent was broken when President Ronald Reagan and his vice president, George Bush, began a new tradition of holding the swearing-in ceremony at the west front.

Before 1937, vice presidents took the oath in the Senate Chamber. Since then, with two exceptions, they have participated in the inaugural ceremonies with the incoming presidents. The exceptions were Gerald Ford and Nelson Rockefeller. These non-elected vice presidents took the oath in the House and Senate Chamber, respectively. The Twenty-fifth Amendment permits the president to nominate, and Congress to confirm, the person to fill a vacancy in the vice presidency.

President Reagan's second inaugural, in 1985, was unusual in several ways. Since the official January 20 date fell on Sunday, he was sworn into office on that day, with the public ceremony held the following day.

The Sunday swearing-in took place near the marble grand staircase in the White House. It was an affair witnessed only by top officials, close personal friends and relatives, plus a small pool of reporters. The event marked the fourth double inaugural; the others were for Hayes, Wilson, and Eisenhower. When the official dates fell on Sundays in 1821 and 1849, the ceremonies for Monroe and for Taylor were postponed to Mondays—the only occasions when this solution was used for the Sunday inaugural problem.

The well-laid plans for the 1985 events were further complicated by devastating weather. A cold spell that dropped the temperature to zero—with a wind chill as low as minus 50º F— forced the swearing-in ceremony to be moved from the west front into the Capitol rotunda. It also prompted the cancellation of the customary parade on Pennsylvania Avenue.

The indoor ceremony on Monday, a historic first for the rotunda, was performed before a standing-room-only audience that included selected citizens and some of the nation's most important officials.

The east front, the previous site for many inaugurations, has a symbolic backdrop that recalls the early days of the republic. On the east portico's pediment above the assembled dignitaries stand three classical female forms

WASHINGTON IN BRONZE *stands against the monumental background of the dome's interior. Figures in the overhead painting—an allegorical glorification of the first president—were drawn as much as 15 feet high to seem life-size from the rotunda floor 180 feet below.*

BRONZE DOORS, *modeled by Randolph Rogers in the 1850s, lead to the rotunda. The doors depict events in the life of Columbus. Below, a visitor studies another bronze door, the entrance to the east portico of the House wing. Designed by Thomas Crawford, the scene portrays George Washington in 1783 bidding farewell to his officers in New York.*

—first sculpted in sandstone and later reproduced in marble—representing America flanked by Justice and Hope.

The theme was inspired by President John Quincy Adams, who pictured Hope as "a Scriptural Image." Her support by an anchor indicated, he wrote, "that this Hope relies upon a Supreme Disposer of events." President Adams rejected a proposal to include Hercules as smacking "too much of the heathen mythology."

Look beyond Adams's pediment and you see the great dome as immobile. But is it? The iron structure moves imperceptibly at the whim of the weather. Scientists once demonstrated that sections of the double-walled, nine-million-pound dome may expand and contract as much as four inches on days with temperature extremes.

At the main east portico on either side of the massive bronze doors leading to the Capitol rotunda are replicas of the statues of War and Peace designed by Luigi Persico, the Italian artist who carried out the pediment adornment.

The sculptured ten-ton bronze doors portray events from the life of Christopher Columbus. Designed in high relief by American sculptor Randolph Rogers, they follow techniques used by Ghiberti and other Italian masters.

Rogers modeled his doors in Rome during the 1850s and had them cast in the Royal Bavarian Foundry of Munich. When installed, the doors opened into the corridor between National Statuary Hall and the new House wing. They were hung at the rotunda entrance in 1871.

The rotunda is at the very heart of the Capitol, and at the hub of streets that lead to it from north, south, east, and west. Here is another example of built-in symbolism, going back to L'Enfant—whose plan put the Capitol at the center of his grid of city streets.

The Capitol's huge circular hall—nearly 100 feet across and more than 180 feet high—also is the heart of the building's historic art displays. From here a maze of rooms and corridors extends into Senate and House wings. Many are filled with sculptures and paintings collected over the years by purchase, gift, or commissions

to various artists.

On the rotunda walls are eight immense oil paintings. Four depict events of the fledgling days of discovery and colonization. One, *The Baptism of Pocahontas* by John Chapman, attracts viewers to its colorful depiction of this scene from the early history of the Virginia colony. Some 200 years after the baptism, one descendant of Pocahontas—the brilliant and erratic John Randolph of Roanoke—sat in Congress as a Virginia representative and senator.

The other four works are priceless links with the American Revolution. Based on sketches made while the leaders were alive, they portray the presentation of the Declaration of Independence, the surrender of Gen. John Burgoyne at Saratoga and of Lord Cornwallis at Yorktown, and General Washington resigning his commission at Annapolis.

Their creator, the artist John Trumbull, had served briefly as an aide to Washington. He knew many of his subjects and traveled far to obtain likenesses. He painted John Adams in London, when the future U.S. president was minister to England. In Paris, amid rumblings of the French Revolution, Trumbull made a portrait of

HEROIC FIGURES *vividly appear in this close-up of the dome's* Apotheosis of Washington. *To cover the 4,664 square feet of concave surface, Constantino Brumidi worked in fresco—paint applied to newly troweled plaster. Brumidi, almost 60, finished his masterpiece in an 11-month period, signing it in 1865. A conservation project completed in 1988 removed grime and overpaint to reveal the fresco's original appearance. Forms in the inner circle represent the 13 original states and the Union; Washington sits between Liberty/Authority and laureled Victory/Fame. Outer groups—clockwise from sword-wielding Freedom—symbolize arts and sciences, the sea, commerce, mechanics, and agriculture.*

ARCHITECT OF THE CAPITOL

GODS AND MORTALS *mingle in the dome's fresco. Ceres rides a reaper as Young America, wearing liberty cap, stands near (top scene, above). Vulcan rests his foot on a cannon (middle scene). Sandaled Mercury offers a bag of gold to Robert Morris, "financier of the Revolution" (bottom scene).*

Bearded Neptune and Aphrodite, holding the Atlantic cable, rise from the sea (top scene, above). Wise Minerva speaks to Benjamin Franklin, Samuel F. B. Morse, and Robert Fulton (middle scene). Armed Freedom—Brumidi's young wife may have been the model—triumphs over Tyranny and Kingly Power (bottom scene).

SCULPTURED SHARPNESS *in wall-flat fresco emblazons the nation's history on the rotunda frieze. Brumidi began it, but died before completing "Penn's Treaty with the Indians." Using Brumidi's sketches, Filippo Costaggini finished the panel and eight others, including "Colonization of New England" (right).*

Thomas Jefferson, then U.S. minister to the French royal government.

"I have been in this capital of dissipation and nonsense near six weeks," Trumbull wrote from Paris to his son Jonathan in 1788, "for the purpose of getting the portraits of the French Officers who were at York Town, and have happily been . . . successfull."

Such human stories, repeated by successive generations of Americans, are like family anecdotes told of favorite ancestors. They breathe spirit into the sculpture around the rotunda's sweeping walls.

One, the tall, commanding figure of Washington, is a bronze copy of Jean-Antoine Houdon's true-to-life statue displayed in the Virginia State Capitol in Richmond.

On either side of Washington stand Jefferson and Hamilton, who made a political bargain that gave the federal capital its Potomac site.

Treasury Secretary Alexander Hamilton was seeking legislation to have the national government assume state debts incurred during the Revolution. Encountering Jefferson near the president's house when New York City was the seat of government, Hamilton persuaded the Virginian to use his influence with southern legislators to win votes for the federal assumption of the state debts. In return, the southerners were offered northern support in placing the Capital in a more central location.

The agreement bore fruit in the act of 1790 that established the government's residence beside the Potomac. But "the Compromise of 1790" brought gibes at the time. One newspaper wrote that "Miss Assumption," beguiled by the promises of "Mr. Residence," had given birth to the child "Potowmacus."

Memories of the War of 1812 cling to the slim bronze statue of Gen. Andrew Jackson, seen in the dashing uniform and cape he wore as the victor of the Battle of New Orleans. Considering the speed of today's communications, it is ironic that neither side knew that peace had been signed on December 24, 1814, two weeks before the January 8, 1815 battle.

(Continued page 85)

ARCHITECT OF THE CAPITOL

CONSTANTINO BRUMIDI *left Rome in his late forties. He had been born there in 1805, studied at the Academy of St. Luke, and gained repute for his murals. Coming to the United States in 1852, he worked more than a quarter-century "to make beautiful the Capitol of the one country on earth in which there is liberty." He almost slipped from a scaffold in 1879 while painting the rotunda frieze, but managed to hold on until help came. The shock, however, hurried his death a few months later. Mathew Brady photographed him with brush and palette in the 1860s.*

LIBRARY OF CONGRESS

77

VISITORS SHRINK *to doll size when seen from the topmost balcony within the dome. Narrow stairs lead to this lofty walkway. Frescoed figures march in an endless band around the rotunda's frieze. The railings just above guard the dome's lower balcony. A camera hung from a rope across the chasm was used to take this picture.*

EVERY SATURDAY, DISTRICT OF COLUMBIA PUBLIC LIBRARY

TOP HATS AND BUSTLES *date tourists of 1871. By the time a visitor climbed to the cupola, said one account, "his collapsed state leaves him in no condition to appreciate" the view.*

EMBARKATION OF THE PILGRIMS *is displayed in the rotunda with seven other historic paintings. Artist Robert Weir shows the group before they set sail from Holland in 1620 for England and the New World.*

SURRENDER OF GENERAL BURGOYNE: *Trumbull portrays British commander John Burgoyne presenting his sword in defeat to Gen. Horatio Gates after the 1777 Battle of Saratoga, a turning point in the Revolutionary War.*

SURRENDER OF LORD CORNWALLIS: *Trumbull portrays Washington's subordinate, Benjamin Lincoln, on the white horse in the center of the painting, accepting the British surrender at Yorktown, October 19, 1781.*

GENERAL GEORGE WASHINGTON RESIGNING HIS COMMISSION, *by Trumbull, shows the Commander in Chief of the Army before Congress at Annapolis, on December 23, 1783. Martha Washington watches from the balcony.*

ARCHITECT OF THE CAPITOL

LANDING OF COLUMBUS: *Artist John Vanderlyn depicts Christopher Columbus landing, October 12, 1492, in the West Indies, on an island that the natives called Guanahani and he named San Salvador.*

BAPTISM OF POCAHONTAS: *John Gadsby Chapman portrays Pocahontas, wearing white, taking the name Rebecca at her baptism prior to her marriage to Englishman John Rolfe. The ceremony in Jamestown, Virginia, is believed to have been in 1613 or 1614.*

DECLARATION OF INDEPENDENCE: *Trumbull's most famous work shows the "Committee of Five"— John Adams, Roger Sherman, Robert Livingston, Benjamin Franklin and Thomas Jefferson — presenting the document to the Continental Congress in 1776.*

DISCOVERY OF THE MISSISSIPPI: *Artist William H. Powell dramatically depicts Spanish conqueror and explorer Hernando de Soto, riding a white horse, the first European to view the Mississippi River, in 1541.*

ARCHITECT OF THE CAPITOL

NATIONAL STATUARY HALL: *Using Samuel F. B. Morse's 1822 painting of the chamber (pages 32-33) as a guide, the staff of the Office of Architect of the Capitol refurbished the hall to look as it did when the House met here until 1857, with the exception of desks, risers, and paint scheme. Five presidents—Madison, Monroe, John Quincy Adams, Jackson, and Fillmore—were inaugurated here. Above the south door is the statue of Liberty and the Eagle (seen at right). Extending a copy of the Constitution in her right hand, the plaster figure of Liberty is flanked by an eagle, representing the U.S., and an entwined serpent, symbolizing wisdom.*

As president in 1835, "Old Hickory" almost lost his life near the spot where his statue now stands. He had attended funeral services for a member of Congress in the House Chamber, and was about to leave the rotunda when a man stepped out from the crowd and aimed a pistol point-blank. The gun misfired. He whipped out a second hidden by his cloak. It, too, misfired in this, the first attempt to assassinate a U.S. president. The assailant was found to be insane.

Another era, the nation's most tragic, comes to mind as you pass the statue of the Civil War general Ulysses S. Grant. "I can't spare this man," Lincoln once replied to Grant's detractors. "He fights."

Today's visitors often stand quietly before a life-size marble statue of Abraham Lincoln in the rotunda. Behind the sculpture lies a charming story told by its creator, Vinnie Ream. A shy 17-year-old, she had begun to attract attention for her talent as a sculptor, and longed to create a likeness of the president. She would later claim that a friend and benefactor, Rep. James Rollins of Missouri, asked Lincoln's permission for her to make sketches in the White House. The president, worried by the war, paid scant attention until Rollins

ARCHITECT OF THE CAPITOL

MARBLE AND BRONZE FIGURES *gaze from atop pedestals in National Statuary Hall. After serving as the House Chamber for nearly 50 years, this room became a showcase in 1864 for statues of state notables. By law each state may place in the Capitol likenesses of two favorite citizens. Above the doorway leading to the rotunda is Clio, the Muse of History (closeup above), riding in a winged chariot and recording passing events. Once the official clock of the House, this timepiece— attached to one of the first neoclassical sculptures to be displayed in a U.S. public building—has marked the minutes since 1819.*

mentioned that the girl was poor. "So she's young and poor, is she. Well, that's nothing agin' her," Lincoln reportedly said. "You may tell her she can come."

Whatever the truth of her story may be, Ream did sculpt a bust of Lincoln that helped convince Congress to award her the commission for the rotunda statue in 1866, making her the first woman to receive a government commission for art.

Once rotunda visitors saw beside the statue a giant head of Lincoln, now moved to the Capitol crypt. The head was fashioned long after Lincoln's death by the noted sculptor Gutzon Borglum. Its powerful characterization came from a profound analysis of Lincoln "looking beyond the queer hat, bad tailoring, and boots you could not now give away," as Borglum commented. "You will find written on his face literally all the complexity of his great nature," the sculptor continued, "half smile, half sadness; half anger, half forgiveness."

(*FAR LEFT AND ABOVE*) ARCHITECT OF THE CAPITOL

In the rotunda, a bereaved nation has paid final tribute to honored individuals, including four murdered presidents—Lincoln, Garfield, McKinley, and Kennedy.

When Kennedy's casket rested here, the lines of mourners stretched 40 blocks. Inside the Capitol, painted figures of the past looked down on ceremonies for the man who had had a special sense of history.

Henry Clay, a member of Congress for 30 years and secretary of state for four, was, in 1852, the first to lie in state in the rotunda. In the post-Civil War years, two fiery opponents of slavery, Rep. Thaddeus Stevens and Sen. Charles Sumner, were accorded the honor. So were Henry Wilson, vice president under Grant, and John Logan, Union Army general and Illinois senator, who formally initiated the Memorial Day observance in 1868.

Peter Charles L'Enfant's disinterred remains were brought here in 1909 in belated recognition of his genius. After L'Enfant came Adm. George Dewey of Manila fame; the Unknown Soldier of World War I; President Warren G. Harding; and Chief Justice and former President William Howard Taft, the only man to hold both offices.

Before sorrowing witnesses lay also the bodies of Gen. John J. Pershing, the commander of the American Expeditionary Forces in World War I, and of the Unknown Soldiers of World War II and Korea, both honored at the same time. In 1953, the tribute went to Sen. Robert

A. Taft, as it had to his father 23 years before. Between 1964 and 1973, Gen. Douglas MacArthur, Sen. Everett M. Dirksen, FBI Director J. Edgar Hoover, and former presidents Herbert C. Hoover, Dwight D. Eisenhower, and Lyndon B. Johnson all lay in state in the Capitol rotunda.

Since 1978, the list of famous Americans who lay in state in the rotunda includes Sen. Hubert Humphrey, who also served as vice president; the Unknown Soldier of the Vietnam Era; Claude Pepper, who served in both the Senate and the House; and presidents Ronald Reagan and Gerald R. Ford. In addition to those who lay in state, three Americans lay in honor in the Capitol rotunda—slain Capitol Police officers Jacob Chestnut and John Gibson in 1998 and Civil Rights pioneer Rosa Parks in 2005.

But sadness has no part in the rotunda's everyday activities. Mostly this room is a place for visitors. "It's like St. Peter's in Rome," tourists sometimes say, looking up into the soaring dome cut by windows through which light filters softly.

Around the dome's eye, 180 feet above the floor, spreads a gigantic allegorical painting by the Italian artist Constantino Brumidi. The painting depicts the apotheosis, or glorification, of George Washington. With Washington in a sweeping circle are delicately colored figures— some 15 feet tall. They include gods and goddesses pictured as protectors of American ideals and progress.

Like much of Brumidi's work in the Capitol, the dome decoration was done in true fresco. In this exacting technique, used by Michelangelo in the Sistine Chapel, an artist applies pigments to fresh plaster. Brumidi, high on a scaffold, had to paint fast, lest the plaster dry and force him to rework a section. To the dedicated artist,

(Continued on page 96)

CORINNE "LINDY" BOGGS CONGRESSIONAL WOMEN'S READING ROOM *once served as the office of the Speaker of the House. On scaffolding in the Hall of Capitols (below) muralist Allyn Cox surveys his work with Lonnelle Aikman, author of* We, the People. *The panel, one of a series completed in 1974, shows Washington and L'Enfant studying a plat on Jenkins Hill, site of the future Capitol.*

ARCHITECT OF THE CAPITOL *(OPPOSITE PAGE)*

FREDERICK MUHLENBERG—*first to be elected Speaker, 1789.*

HENRY CLAY *molded the office to its powerful role.*

SAM RAYBURN *served longest— 17 years. The Speaker is second in sucession to the presidency.*

SPEAKER'S LOBBY *is located just off the floor of the House Chamber. The long, ornate hallway is lined with the official portraits of former Speakers of the House. The Speaker is the residing officer of the House of Representatives.*

ARCHITECT OF THE CAPITOL *(opposite page)*

THE HOUSE OF REPRESENTATIVES CHAMBER *(pages 92-93) is one of the largest legislative halls in the world. The House held its first meeting in the new House wing on December 16, 1857. Here, in its stately new quarters, the 35th Congress spent months in heated debate on the question of whether to admit Kansas as a free state or as a slave state. As House membership grew, rows of seats replaced desks; mahogany tables now provide working space for the leadership on both sides of the chamber. Traditionally, Republicans sit to the right and Democrats to the left facing the Speaker. Above the gallery doors, 23 relief portraits of noted lawgivers from the Babylonian king Hammurabi to Thomas Jefferson remind members of their mission. State seals border the ceiling. Behind the Speaker's rostrum, Missouri marble accents the room's walnut paneling. Two paintings adorn the chamber: Marquis de Lafayette by Ary Scheffer, 1823, and George Washington by John Vanderlyn, 1834.*

HOUSE OF REPRESENTATIVES - *The Speaker of the House presides from the highest dais in the center the tables in the third row of the chamber.*

of the House of Representatives Chamber. Leaders of the Republican Party and the Democratic Party use

HOUSE MEMBERS' RETIRING ROOM *is located just off the Speaker's Lobby. Gilt ceilings and ornate pilasters contribute to the elaborate decor. Original to the room's construction in the 1850s, the Minton tile floor patterns are designed to resemble oriental carpets.*

LIBRARY OF CONGRESS

CONSTITUENTS *buttonhole members in the Speaker's Lobby (above). The taller figure at left is possibly Speaker Thomas Brackett Reed, whose portrait is shown on the back wall at right. Today, only members, reporters, and select staff have access to the lobby.*

WALNUT PANELING *enriches the Rayburn House Reception Room (below). In a special niche stands a 5½-foot Sèvres vase, one of four given to the House and Senate by France in 1918.*

DRAMATIC HIGH-CEILING CORRIDOR

on the first floor of House wing, the Hall of Columns takes it name from the 28 fluted white marble columns that line the hallway. The modified Corinthian capitals, designed by Thomas U. Walter, incorporate tobacco leaves with acanthus and thistles. Since 1976 the hall has housed statues from the National Statuary Hall Collection, currently including Stephen Austin, Francis Preston Blair, Saint Damien, James Harlan, Philip Kearny, John E. Kenna, Esther Hobart Morris, Florence R. Sabin, James Shields, and John Winthrop.

however, no challenge was too difficult for his adopted country.

Born in Rome of Greek and Italian parents, Constantino Brumidi had left his homeland in 1852 and found refuge in the United States. He worked between 1855 and 1880 to decorate the Capitol's interior with vivid, patriotic, and classical designs.

"C. Brumidi, artist. Citizen of the U.S.," he signed his huge mural on the surrender at Yorktown, now in the House restaurant. "My one ambition," he wrote, ". . . is that I may live long enough to make beautiful the Capitol of the one country on earth in which there is liberty."

Brumidi was 60 when he finished the dome canopy, and 72 when he began work on his circular frieze presenting scenes from American history. He had completed six panels and was proceeding on the seventh, "Penn's Treaty with the Indians," when his chair slipped on the scaffold. Desperately he grabbed hold of the scaffold and clung—58 feet from the floor—until rescuers came.

He died several months later, and Congress commissioned artist Filippo Costaggini to complete the panels. Costaggini spent eight years translating to full scale the remaining small sketches left by Brumidi.

Still unfinished in 1889 was a 31-foot gap, which was not filled in until 1953 by Allyn Cox of New York. His subjects: the Civil War, the Spanish-American War, and the Birth of Aviation, illustrated by the Wright brothers' flight at Kitty Hawk, N.C., in 1903.

Approaching and entering nearby National Statuary Hall, the visitor comes upon a unique collection of bronze and marble statues. Presented by the states in memory of distinguished

ARCHITECT OF THE CAPITOL

citizens, these figures honor pioneers, missionaries, teachers, soldiers, inventors, and others who made contributions to state and country.

Here, in commanding pose, stands Ethan Allen, Vermont's Revolutionary War hero who, according to tradition, demanded the surrender of Ticonderoga "in the name of the Jehovah and the Continental Congress."

Across the room sits a thoughtful young man examining a model of a steamboat—Robert Fulton of Pennsylvania.

The name "John Gorrie M.D.," carved on one of the statues contributed by Florida, identifies the ingenious doctor who patented the first ice-making machine in 1851, after experimenting with devices to cool the rooms of his fevered patients

The inventor of the Cherokee syllabary, Sequoyah, memorialized in bronze by Oklahoma, was the first Native American added to the National Statuary Hall Collection. The first woman honored, temperance pioneer and educator Frances E. Willard, is represented in a marble likeness donated by Illinois.

Some of the men commemorated in marble and bronze on pedestals lining the walls of National Statuary Hall were members of Congress who knew this room well during its half century as the House Chamber. Clay, Houston, and Webster sat as representatives here. Clay served as Speaker, ruling from the throne-like chair on a platform canopied in crimson and green draperies.

The transformation of the former Hall of the House into a national hall of fame began more than a century ago, after it had become, in the words of a legislative committee, "worse than uselessly occupied as a place of storage and traffic." It was "draped in cobwebs and carpeted with dust," said Rep. Justin S. Morrill of Vermont in debate on the resolution to turn it into an exhibit hall.

"I look to see where Calhoun sat . . . and where Clay sat and I find a woman selling oranges and root beer," remarked a colleague in supporting the measure.

As passed in July 1864, the bill cleared out the hucksters, and authorized the president to invite each state to contribute two statues of outstanding deceased citizens.

First to arrive—from Rhode Island in 1870—was a statue of Nathanael Greene, fighting quartermaster general in the Revolution, who poured out his own fortune to supply needy soldiers. Gradually others followed, until finally their combined weight in the early 1930s raised fears that the whole assemblage might crash through the floor. Since then the number of statues in the room has been reduced. Others of the collection now stand in the Hall of Columns on the House side and throughout the Capitol.

As of 2005, every state had contributed two statues to the Capitol's roster of state notables. A law passed in 2000 authorized any state to replace a statue, provided the state bear all costs associated with the new statue and removing the replaced statue. Kansas selected former president and World War II commander Dwight David Eisenhower in 2003 in place of George Washington Glick. California chose former

President Ronald Reagan to replace Thomas Starr King in 2009. The statue of former President Gerald Ford of Michigan replaced that of Zachariah Chandler in 2011.

Nine women have been honored—Helen Keller (Alabama) is the most recent. Not until 1959 did the second woman join the 1905 statue of Frances Willard. Wyoming chose Esther Hobart Morris, who made history as the world's first woman justice of the peace, and who helped persuade Wyoming to become the first state to adopt woman suffrage. Minnesota immortalized Maria Sanford, educator and civic

98

leader—called the "best-loved woman" in her state. Colorado sent a likeness of Dr. Florence Rena Sabin, the first woman member of the National Academy of Sciences.

Washington State added another tribute to a woman—Mother Joseph, a Catholic nun who made valuable contributions to health care, education, and social work in the Northwest. In 1985, Montana donated a statue of Jeannette Rankin, the first woman to serve in Congress and a dedicated pacifist who voted against U.S. entry into World Wars I and II.

Two of the most recent statues to enter the

DELEGATES SIGN *the Constitution after its final drafting, September 17, 1787. The painting, acquired by Congress in 1940, hangs at the east stairway of the House wing. Artist Howard Chandler Christy worked in a navy sail loft on the 20-by-30-foot canvas. It shows George Washington, presiding, with the Constitution's framers in Independence Hall. Alexander Hamilton talks to Benjamin Franklin (with cane). James Madison, the document's chief architect, sits at the table to Franklin's left.*

collection honor Native American women. North Dakota's Sakakawea, added in 2003, honors the famous Lewis and Clark Expedition guide, depicted with her infant son strapped on her back. The author of the first book by a Native American woman, Sarah Winnemucca, is shown holding a book and a shellflower—the origin of her Paiute name. Nevada donated her statue to National Statuary Hall in 2005.

The Capitol also exhibits a statue of Oklahoma's famous cowboy humorist, Will Rogers, who loved to josh the members of what he called the Washington "joke factory." When the politicians "get in that immense Hall," wrote Will, "they begin to get Serious, and it's then that they do such Amusing things."

Nor is Will Rogers the only cowboy to be corralled among the frock-coated statesmen and uniformed generals in the nation's hall of fame.

ARCHITECT OF THE CAPITOL

DR. MARTIN LUTHER KING, JR., *the bronze bust by sculptor John Wilson, was unveiled in the rotunda on January 16, 1986, the 57th anniversary of the civil rights leader's birth.*

Not far away stands a seven-foot statue of Montana's roving cowboy-artist Charles Marion Russell, who recorded a dying era of men and beasts in the Old West.

"You never saw one of his paintings," Rogers wrote of his friend's work, "that you couldn't tell just what the Indian, the Horse and Buffalo were thinking about."

Ceremonies in the rotunda usually accompany each statue presentation. Alaska made one gift in 1971, another in 1977. In turn, the state saluted former U.S. Sen. E. L. "Bob" Bartlett, called the "Architect of Alaska Statehood," and Sen. Ernest Gruening, former governor and noted author.

Though Massachusetts has donated no statue of John Quincy Adams, a small bronze marker in National Statuary Hall has honored his memory since 1888.

The engraved plaque was set into the floor at the spot where a stroke felled Adams at his desk on February 21, 1848. He died in the Speaker's office two days later, after 17 years of service as a highly respected member of the House following his single term as president.

By coincidence, the Adams plaque also marks the best place for guides to demonstrate the chamber's acoustics. Standing at its location, you can hear a whisper from across the room, though it is barely audible close by.

Another of the plaques was installed in the floor of National Statuary Hall in 1974. This marker identifies the site of the desk used by Abraham Lincoln. It commemorates, as well, his term in the House as an Illinois representative from 1847 to 1849.

Congress later placed plaques with the names of six other representatives who achieved the presidency and who also sat in the Old House Chamber: John Tyler, James K. Polk, Millard Fillmore, Franklin Pierce, James Buchanan, and Andrew Johnson.

In another phase of the restoration program that evokes National Statuary Hall's past as the House Chamber, gold-fringed red draperies

(Continued page 104)

IN THE CRYPT, *a chandelier hangs above the compass stone that marks the center of the Capitol, the zero point from which Washington, D.C.'s streets are numbered and lettered.*

VISITORS' HEADS *create a living frieze around a balustrade in the Senate rotunda. Architect Latrobe built this vestibule as a light well replacing stairs burned in the British raid of 1814. He gave capitals atop the 16 columns a motif of tobacco flowers and leaves— tribute to the plant's importance in the young nation's economy.*

NATHANAEL GREENE, *Revolutionary War hero, stands in stone in the Capitol— the first statue to be placed after states were invited thus to honor noted citizens.*

RHODE ISLAND

ARCHITECT OF THE CAPITOL

103

accent its columns—as shown in the 1822 paint-ing (page 32) by Samuel F. B. Morse.

Still other details that recall history and by-gone lifestyles include the room's four reopened fireplaces, an 1819 engraving of the Declaration of Independence, and a copy of the three-tiered oil lamp chandelier.

In addition to the state statues, Congress has collected more than 500 other works of art, from portraits and panoramic paintings to individual statues and busts—including those of presi-dents, vice presidents, chief justices, and Indian chiefs.

At every turn you see faces—severe or benign, young or old. They recall a saying by Ralph Waldo Emerson: "There is properly no history, only biography."

Presidential likenesses scattered about the building are the easiest to identify. Some are famous works, like Thomas Sully's paintings of Jefferson and Jackson and the portraits of George Washington by Charles Willson Peale

and Gilbert Stuart.

Others record important historic events—such as Lincoln meeting with his cabinet to read the Emancipation Proclamation, a scene depicted in the huge painting over the Senate's west stairway. The artist, Francis B. Carpenter, did the painting in the White House; the presi-dent himself authenticated details.

Twenty of the busts in the collection of vice presidents look out from niches around the walls of the Senate Chamber gallery—a reminder that the chief official duty of this officer is to preside as president of the Senate.

John Adams, in ruffled stock, is here as vice president under Washington. Adams was far from pleased by his election. He wrote his wife that his country had arranged for him "the most insignificant office that ever the invention of man contrived."

"I have now . . . 'taken the veil,'" Theodore Roosevelt wrote a friend after his election to the post in 1900.

REVOLUTIONARY WAR GENERAL
David Wooster, mortally wounded in 1777 at Ridgefield, Connecticut, inspired Brumidi's fresco for a Senate Appropriations Committee room. Hundreds of Brumidi murals adorn the Capitol.

Chester A. Arthur, also among the 20 busts in the Senate gallery, served as vice president for only six months in 1881 before Garfield's assassination brought him the presidency. Political enemies called him "His Accidency," a nickname shared with two previous vice presidents, Millard Fillmore and John Tyler, who ascended to the presidency following the death of the incumbent.

Only two vice presidents have ever resigned. John C. Calhoun gave up the office in 1832 to return to the Senate. Spiro T. Agnew, after pleading "no contest" to charges of income-tax evasion, stepped down in 1973.

As for the Indian chiefs, three busts in the Capitol go back to the 1850s, when tribal leaders often traveled to the seat of government to sign land treaties or to seek redress for grievances. Two of these figures represent the same man—a Chippewa chief called Be shekee, or "the Buffalo." The marble original, displayed in the Senate wing, was sculpted in 1854 by

Francis Vincenti. The bronze version, seen on the House side, was made four years later in the Capitol's bronze shop by Joseph Lassalle.

It took diligent detective work a century ago to identify a mysterious third bust, also by Vincenti. It turned out to be that of another Chippewa chief, Aysh-ke-bah-ke-ko-zhay, known as "Flat Mouth."

Even more engaging than the Indian busts is a seven-ton block of marble in the rotunda. This monument, surmounted by heads of three notable 19th-century American women, once stood in the crypt amid massive columns and groined arches that support the rotunda floor

WASHINGTON OUTSIDE AND INSIDE,
DISTRICT OF COLUMBIA PUBLIC LIBRARY

GLIDED SPLENDOR: *Brumidi frescoes and Minton tiles decorate the Senate Reception Room. Portraits by subsequent artists depict great senators of the past. At left, an 1873 engraving shows the room as the Ladies' Parlor.*

was left in the rotunda floor to admit light to the crypt below.

"The idea was poetical, grand, and captivating," said John Trumbull. But after his paintings of the Revolution were hung in 1826, he found that damp air rising from the crypt was ruining his work. At Trumbull's urging, Capitol masons closed the floor opening in 1828. Four years later, Washington's heirs decided against removing the general's remains from the tomb at Mount Vernon.

Congress then commissioned Horatio Greenough to make a statue of the Father of His Country. Greenough draped his marble Washington in classic Greek style, a sight that shocked the public when the statue was first displayed in the rotunda in 1841.

As architect Charles Bulfinch had predicted, people wanted "to see the great man as their imagination had painted him." He feared that the statue would "give the idea of entering or leaving a bath." The heroic 20-ton figure was moved out to the grounds; then, in 1908, it was transferred to the Smithsonian Institution.

Washington's tomb site once held a black-draped bier. On this somber catafalque, first built for Lincoln, have rested the bodies of those who have lain in state in the rotunda since 1865. The catafalque is now on display in the Capitol Visitor Center.

On the ground floor of the Senate wing are colorful tile floors and decorative murals that cover wall and ceiling surfaces of corridors and committee rooms.

(Continued on page 110)

above. The work honors women's rights pioneers Lucretia Mott, Elizabeth Cady Stanton, and Susan B. Anthony.

The portrait monument to the pioneers of the women's suffrage movement was presented to the Capitol by the National Woman's Party in 1921. Representatives of more than seventy women's organizations attended the unveiling ceremony. Hundreds of women celebrated in the rotunda, waving banners in the happy knowledge that they had recently won their long battle for women's suffrage.

Two floors below the portrait monument, and beneath the center of the rotunda, visitors find a never-used tomb. After George Washington's death, Congress authorized a monument to honor the first president at the heart of the future Capitol. His remains were to be transferred from Mount Vernon and placed in a space beneath the monument. But years passed without action.

About 1820, during construction of the central section of the Capitol, a wide circular opening

SENATE CHAMBER—*Busts of several past vice presidents occupy niches in the gallery bench seating, the Senate Chamber is furnished with desks, 48 of which were ordered in 1819.*

ARCHITECT OF THE CAPITOL

walls of the Senate Chamber. Unlike in the House of Representatives Chamber, which has The Senate first met in this chamber on January 4, 1859.

U. S. SENATE COLLECTION

LACQUERED SNUFFBOXES,
though no longer used, sit on ledges
near the Senate rostrum.

CRYSTAL SHAKER *dispenses*
blotting sand, a heritage of days when
senators wrote with quill pens. Today
the desktop shakers stand empty.

The multi-colored encaustic tiles were made in the mid-1850s by skilled craftsmen of England's Minton works. Though millions visitors have trod these tiles, even worn them down in spots, the colors and intricate patterns remain amazingly vivid.

On the walls and corridor ceilings, Brumidi painted in oil, tempera, and fresco. Laboring for years, he created incredibly varied designs of birds, animals, flowers, and fruits, interlaced with scrollwork. He painted trompe l'oeil medallion portraits of many famous Americans, intermingled with battle scenes, landscapes, and panels representing farming and industry.

Outside the room once used by the Committee on Patents, you see Brumidi's portraits of Benjamin Franklin in his laboratory, and of rival inventors Robert Fulton and John Fitch with early steamboat models.

In the hall that leads from the Patent Corridor are more Brumidi murals, and—two 20th-century events—a mural by Allyn Cox that depicts the 1969 moon landing and Charles Schmidt's mural of the ill-fated space shuttle *Challenger* and crew.

Down the main north-south corridor is the restored Old Supreme Court Chamber off the small Senate rotunda in the oldest part of the Capitol. This area, occupied by the Senate from 1800 to 1810, and by the Supreme Court from 1810 to 1860, knew events that rocked the country and helped mold its destiny.

Here, in the early Senate Chamber in 1801 and 1805, Jefferson was sworn in as the third U.S. president, and here, in 1857, Chief Justice Roger B. Taney read his opinion in the Dred Scott case, which denied citizenship to people of African descent and fanned the fires of controversy that soon exploded into the Civil War.

SENATE LOBBY *recalls rooms of the past where individuals with pet projects buttonholed legislators in attempts to influence legislation. From such anteroom meetings came the term "lobbying." Today, senators enjoy privacy in their lobby since it ranks as part of the Senate floor, an area where rules limit public access. Clockwise from left in this 1985 photograph are senators Strom Thurmond, William S. Cohen, Thad Cochran, Edward M. Kennedy, Howell T. Heflin, and Russell B. Long.*

Displaying much of its original furniture and decoration, the court chamber has been restored to its appearance during the mid-19th century. Particularly striking is its half-dome ceiling—the "umbrella vault" designed by Benjamin Henry Latrobe when he created a room for the Senate on the second floor.

Even in the days when both the Capitol and the nation were young, however, the ground floor space allotted to the high court was uncomfortably crowded.

It was "hardly capacious enough for a ward justice," wrote a New York correspondent in 1824. "It is a triangular, semicircular, odd-shaped apartment, with three windows, and a profusion of arches. . . . Owing to the smallness . . . the Judges are compelled to put on their robes in the presence of spectators."

But the cases heard by the court were of national significance, and fashionable Washington found in lawyers' eloquence a substitute for its lack of the glamour and cultural diversions of the big city.

Here Webster in 1819 argued an important constitutional issue involving his alma mater, Dartmouth College, and ended with the moving words: "It is, Sir . . . a small college and yet there are those who love it."

Capitol architect George M. White and his staff—working with the Senate Commission on Art and Antiquities in the 1970s—restored the no-less historic Old Senate Chamber above that of the Old Supreme Court.

Again the room looks as it did in the 1850s. Replicas of desks used then stand in their original spots. The visitors' gallery overlooks the floor, and the original carved and gilded eagle spreads its wings above the chair of the president of the Senate.

In the formative years of the nation's territorial and economic expansion, this room echoed furious debates over guiding legislation. It heard Sen. Thomas Corwin of Ohio make his brave, futile stand in 1847 against popular sentiment for the Mexican War. And it saw Corwin's prophecy come true that acquiring land from

MARBLE ROOM

adjoins the Senate Lobby as part of the Senate floor. The decorative ceiling, pilasters, and fluted Corinthian columns of white Italian marble contrast with Tennessee marble walls and wainscoting. The elegant room is a private area for senators. In the Brumidi Corridor, Allyn Cox's mural (right) records mankind's giant leap in 1969, when U.S. astronauts Neil Armstrong and Edwin Aldrin became the first men to set foot on the moon.

U. S. SENATE COLLECTION

Mexico would lead to disastrous sectional strife.

Indeed, it was in this very room, less than ten years later, that congressional conflict over the extension of slavery in the new western lands reached a climax in the brutal caning of Sen. Charles Sumner of Massachusetts by South Carolina Rep. Preston S. Brooks.

The Civil War was still an ominous shadow in 1859 when the Senate moved in ceremonial procession to its present chamber in the new Senate wing.

The following year, the Supreme Court took over the former Senate Chamber, where the justices would remain for three-quarters of a century before moving on to their own new building in 1935.

Meanwhile, Brumidi was continuing his labor of love during the 1860s and early 1870s, continuing his work on two of the Capitol's most impressive showrooms, located behind the Senate Chamber at either end of the senators' private lobby.

In the President's Room, Brumidi painted his own art gallery on square inch after square inch of ceiling and walls. In addition to panels showing portraits of Washington's first cabinet, he painted designs framing symbolic figures, pensive Madonna-like figures, happy cherubs, and four historical persons, including Christopher Columbus and Benjamin Franklin.

Though presidents seldom visit this room now, many chief executives, beginning in the 1860s, used the room to sign bills into law near the close of congressional sessions.

Equally ornate is the Senate Reception Room, where senators meet constituents. But how, you may ask, did portraits of past notables painted in recent times get into the frames made long before by Brumidi?

The story goes back to 1874. "Sooner or later," the artist declared, the spaces that remained among his panels "must be completed."

The time came in 1957, when a special Senate committee, headed by future president John F. Kennedy, chose five outstanding senators to be honored by portraits painted in the medallions.

The selection was "nearly an impossible task," Senator Kennedy wrote at the time. In the end the committee recommended five: the "Great Triumvirate," Clay, Webster, and Calhoun, and leaders of later progressive and conservative forces—Robert M. La Follette, Sr., and Robert A. Taft.

In 2004, portraits of former senators Arthur H. Vandenberg and Robert F. Wagner were added to the "Famous Five" in the Senate Reception Room. Two years later a scene of Roger Sherman and Oliver Ellsworth framing the Connecticut compromise at the 1787 Constitutional Convention brought to nine the number of outstanding senators honored.

In 1970 the nonprofit U. S. Capitol Historical Society offered to donate the necessary funds, together with the talent of Allyn Cox, to produce a series of decorative murals in the House wing. Congress accepted and by midsummer of 1974 the first corridor was completed by Cox and his chief assistant, Cliff Young. The second corridor was finished in 1982, and the third—from Cox's designs—was executed by EverGreene Painting Studios in 1993–94.

Visitors to the ground floor corridors in the House wing can now look up to vaulted ceilings and see vivid pictures of personalities and events from American history.

THE HALL OF CAPITOLS, the first Cox corridor, has portraits of the first nine

THE PRESIDENT'S ROOM, *one of the most ornate chambers in the Capitol, recalls bygone years when the chief executive would come here to sign bills into law. The elaborate frescoes and murals are the work of Brumidi. The portrait in the far wall panel depicts Henry Knox, who served as secretary of war under George Washington; epaulets recall his combat role during the Revolutionary War.*

architects of the Capitol and paintings of the buildings where Congress met. Here, too, are eight large murals depicting such scenes as George Washington laying the Capitol's cornerstone, the burning of the building by British invaders in 1814, and the rotunda when it served as a Civil War hospital.

Funded by the Daughters of the American Revolution, the second corridor, the Great Experiment Hall, was finished in 1983. Its subjects illustrate 300 years of events related to legislation by Congress.

The selection of the Mayflower Compact to introduce this series was based on history's judgment that the accord was a pioneering step toward self-government in what would eventually become the United States.

In his drawing, Cox pictures a group of the signers of the compact as they gathered in the cramped cabin of the Pilgrim ship before landing at Plymouth in 1620.

The agreement itself provided that the quarreling and often divided *Mayflower* passengers would form a "civill body politick" and abide by the laws adopted for the general good of Plymouth Colony.

By 1982, when muralist Cox died at age 86, he had left a legacy that unrolls a pageant of memorable events. On either side of each scene are vignettes that show the human and everyday side of life from that particular era.

Vignettes accompanying the Mayflower Compact portray a woman at her spinning wheel, and an Indian chief as a reminder to us of the original Americans who would meet the arriving immigrants.

Everywhere, in both large and smaller paintings, you see details that give authenticity and vitality to the work.

Clothing, furnishings, and outdoor background all had to be precise in period and situation. Like a sculptor, Cox studied the physical characteristics of his human subjects to ensure correct height, weight, and proper hang of clothing. Here, in Benjamin Franklin's garden—where Cox placed delegates discussing

the drafting of the Constitution in 1787— find the slight figure of James Madison beside Franklin. Over there, George Washington (six-feet-two) dominates the scene as he takes the oath of office in 1789 on the balcony of the temporary capital of New York.

The chronologically arranged paintings attract passing visitors. They see President Monroe and his cabinet of 1823 devising the far-reaching Monroe Doctrine that would warn European nations against further colonization or interference in the Western Hemisphere.

They observe Abraham Lincoln, at the east front of the Capitol in 1865, delivering his second inaugural address—the speech that contained the famous appeal "to bind up the nation's wounds . . . and cherish a just, and a lasting peace."

Capturing a more flamboyant mood, Cox painted "Teddy" Roosevelt campaigning for the presidency, while H. L. Mencken and other reporters scribble notes.

Early American industry is represented by an 1868 iron foundry with men putting a product through a heat-treatment process. Vignettes of women factory workers and a cotton gin contribute to the theme of the Industrial Revolution. Across the corridor, a steam-powered boat suggests America's transportation expansion by river and canal.

Finally, Cox spotlights the end of an era in a painting of suffrage marchers parading in 1917—three years before the 19th amendment gave women nationwide voting rights.

In 1993–1994 the Westward Expansion corridor, the final series of murals based on Cox's designs, was completed by EverGreene Painting Studios. Maps, historical scenes, and colorful vignettes echoing Cox's style provide a sweeping panorama of the nation's westward expansion and settlement.

Yet, however beguiling such historic murals and other forms of Capitol art may be, sightseeing visitors come sooner or later to the legislative chambers in which members of Congress speak and vote.

VICE PRESIDENTIAL BUST COLLECTION

Marble busts of former vice presidents are displayed in the Senate wing. Seen here, clockwise from top left, are the busts of John Adams by Daniel Chester French, Adlai E. Stevenson by Franklin Simmons, Garret A. Hobart by F. Edwin Elwell, Henry Wilson by Daniel Chester French, and (center) Gerald R. Ford by Walker Hancock.

JOHN ADAMS, *first vice president, cast a record 29 tie-breaking votes as president of the Senate, the vice president's principal constitutional role.*

HENRY WILSON, *the shoemaker who became senator, served as Grant's vice president from March 4, 1873 until his death from a stroke in the Capitol in 1875.*

ADLAI E. STEVENSON, *senator from Illinois and later vice president under Cleveland (1893–97), was praised for presiding over the Senate in a dignified, nonpartisan manner.*

GARRET A. HOBART *became the 24th vice president in 1897 but died in office two years later from a heart attack. He was succeeded by Theodore Roosevelt.*

HENRY WILSON

GERALD R. FORD *served as 40th vice president from 1973 to 1974. Ford had served 25 years in the House, eight as Republican leader. Appointed vice president following the resignation of Spiro Agnew, he became the 38th president when Richard Nixon resigned in 1974. As president, he sought to calm the passions of the post-Watergate era, while cautioning that he was "a Ford, not a Lincoln."*

U. S. SENATE COLLECTION

U. S. SENATE COLLECTION

JOHN JAY *served as chief justice of the United States from 1789 to 1795, after notable contributions to the peace agreement ending the American Revolution.*

JOHN MARSHALL, *chief justice of the United States (1801 to 1835), helped mold the Supreme Court and the nation with far-reaching opinions.*

U. S. SENATE COLLECTION

The House Chamber—139 feet long and 93 feet wide—is one of the world's largest legislative rooms. Here representatives sit in rows of unmarked fixed seats, as if in a theater without reserved seating. By tradition, however, Republicans group themselves to the Speaker's left and Democrats to the right.

In the smaller Senate Chamber, each member has an assigned desk. Here too the Republicans and Democrats sit respectively to the left and right of the vice president. Each desk has an inkwell and a crystal shaker to hold blotting sand—mementos of the quill-pen era. And on ledges flanking the rostrum rest two lacquered snuffboxes, recalling the sneezes that many old-time senators considered an induce-

OLD SUPREME COURT CHAMBER, *contains many original furnishings. Busts of the first chief justices look down on the vaulted hall designed by architect Latrobe. The "pumpkin shell" ceiling, rebuilt after the Capitol was burned by the British, supports the Old Senate Chamber above. Beginning in 1810, counselors, including Daniel Webster, argued constitutional cases here. The Supreme Court relocated upstairs (right) after the Senate moved to its present-day quarters in 1859.*

U. S. SENATE COMMISSION ON ART

ENGRAVING FROM "PICTURESQUE WASHINGTON," DISTRICT OF COLUMBIA PUBLIC LIBRARY

CHERUB AND EAGLE

grace bronze railings of members' staircases in both the Senate and House wings. A French sculptor living in Philadelphia, Edmond Baudin, modeled them in 1859 from designs by Brumidi. The latter worked on Capitol murals from 1855 to 1880.

ment to clear-headed eloquence. For a modern touch, microphones are now used by the senators to amplify their remarks and rebuttals.

Visiting constituents, who may wonder at the casual atmosphere or lack of attendance in today's chambers, are reassured to learn that most of the labors of Congress are performed in committees. As Woodrow Wilson wrote, "Congress in session is Congress on public exhibition, whilst Congress in its committee rooms is Congress at work."

Important legislation, however, brings senators and representatives hurrying to record their yeas or nays.

But there is still another side to the Capitol, behind the corridors, legislative chambers, and the public activities of Congress. You find this side in a working world of men and women whose job behind the scenes is to preserve and maintain the vast home of Congress.

BRILLIANT TRACERY

surrounds the North Brumidi Corridor on the ground floor of the Senate wing. Here the artist and his assistants painted walls and ceilings with birds, flowers, medallion portraits, and important inventions. Minton tiles pave the floor.

ARCHITECT OF THE CAPITOL

The Capitol at Work

"THE CAPITOL is a little city in itself," wrote a knowledgeable Washington newspaperman, Frank G. Carpenter, back in 1883.

It still is, only more so, as congressional chores expand to meet the increasing demands of modern legislation.

Within the expansive Capitol complex, which includes nearby office buildings, there are carpentry, plumbing, electrical, and machine-repair shops; purchasing offices, barbershops, gymnasiums, beauty parlors, libraries, stationery shops, and mailing rooms.

A medical staff maintains first-aid and consulting rooms, mainly for members of Congress, but available to outsiders in case of serious accident or other emergency. The United States Capitol Police, established in 1828 and responsible to a congressional board, guards the buildings and grounds.

There is a Capitol Prayer Room, created by a concurrent resolution of House and Senate in 1954. The nondenominational chamber remains open around the clock when Congress is in session. Anonymous donors presented the room's Bible, U.S. flag, and stained glass window showing George Washington kneeling in prayer.

Many senators and representatives come to this room of meditation and prayer. And the number increases, attendants report, when crucial bills are up for decision.

"The late Senator Carter Glass once said that in 28 years he had never known a speech to change a vote," one member noted. "But I know of several colleagues whose votes changed after visits to our Prayer Room."

Congress's working quarters are scattered from its debating halls to the farthest corners of its office buildings.

Immediately surrounding the formal chambers are the legislators' private lobbies and cloakrooms, while beyond stretch mazes of administrative and clerical offices.

The word "lobbyist" came from such legislative anterooms, in which special pleaders sought to influence lawmakers. The term "lobbying" was current in the Capitol at least as early as 1832. During the heyday of railway expansion, the practice was so effective that Vermont's Senator Justin S. Morrill once sarcastically proposed appointing a committee to consult with a railway president waiting in another lobby, to learn whether or not he wished any further legislation.

Rules for admitting outsiders to the floors of House and Senate have varied sharply through the years. During Senate debates on the Missouri Compromise in 1820, gallant Vice President Daniel D. Tompkins invited so many ladies into the chamber that they filled all the available seats and "got literally on the floor, to the no small inconvenience and displeasure of many gentlemen," a commentator reported.

When Congress is in session today, only officially authorized persons may come onto either floor. All others are rigidly excluded—not only from where Congress sits, but from most adjoining rooms as well.

Though Congress is proud of its splendid rooms, lawmaking, after all, is its basic function. Members have their own office staffs, usually including an administrative assistant, legislative assistants, and secretarial and clerical help. Each member also can turn to the Congressional Research Service of the Library of Congress for information on any subject.

The committees that members may serve on—Congress has 36 standing committees plus

PRAYER ROOM *stays open at all times to legislators from both houses during sessions. The stained glass window depicts General George Washington kneeling in prayer.*

ARCHITECT OF THE CAPITOL

STATELY ELEGANCE: *Several congressional committees have meeting rooms in the Capitol, but few can match the splendor of the ornate Senate Appropriations Committee hearing room. Decorated in the Pompeian style by Constantino Brumidi, the room was originally designed for the Senate Naval Affairs Committee, which explains the naval instruments—anchor, chart, compass, sextant—held by the "floating maidens" painted on the walls.*

hundreds of subcommittees—employ batteries of technical people to advise on anything from flood control to space flight. In addition, the Senate and House have legislative and administrative staffs—headed by the secretary of the Senate and clerk of the House—that include document superintendents, financial clerks, librarians, and others. Their knowledge of congressional functions and traditions is essential.

Yet despite such assistance, only members can attend to many matters. They must see visiting constituents, gather information, and perform other services for state and business interests back home. Responding to letters is a big item. Millions of letters and emails pour into the Capitol complex annually. Constituents may ask for help with problems involving Social Security or welfare benefits, a government job, or advice on how to find a runaway spouse or child. A would-be inventor once asked his congressman to send him a list of everything that had not yet been invented.

Letters from constituents may contain bouquets of praise, or more frequently, brickbats. Occasionally, the temptation to talk back is overwhelming. One representative contented himself with two words in replying to an irate constituent who had threatened to move to Canada. "Bon voyage," he wrote.

Another part of the job is the time-honored practice of sending out government bulletins on subjects ranging from farm machinery and baby

PHOTOGRAPH BY OFFICE OF PHOTOGRAPHY, U.S. HOUSE OF REPRESENTATIVES, COURTESY OFFICE OF THE SPEAKER

HOUSE OF REPRESENTATIVES PAGES *pause for a group photograph in the Capitol rotunda with Speaker of the House Nancy Pelosi.*

care to gun control and nuclear energy.

As sessions of Congress run longer and longer, members lean heavily on modern communications to keep in touch with the people back home. Newsletters and member web sites keep constituents informed.

For other media connections to home districts, the Capitol houses radio and TV recording facilities for legislators to use at cost. In convenient studios, members prepare their reports to constituents. The tapes and films go to local broadcast stations.

With all these activities, members have crowded schedules. In the early years of this century, Congress sometimes met for only nine months of the 24-month session. Mail then con-

cerned mostly personal and routine interests, such as free-seed distribution, rural routes, pensions—and now and again some special piece of legislation.

Today, members meet almost continuously and consider masses of legislation suggested in presidential messages, executive department reports, or petitions from private groups or individuals. They must be ready to defend voting stands to constituents who have greater access than ever before to information.

You could write a book (people have) on how a proposal becomes law, sometimes by more than 20 stages. The House and Senate go about the business differently. But, shorn of details, the basic steps are these: In the House, for

ARCHITECT OF THE CAPITOL

CAPITOL POLICE *officers, uniformed and carrying hickory canes, posed at the Capitol for this 1860s photograph.*

example, a member drafts a bill—say, one on energy—and drops it into the clerk's "hopper." The parliamentarian picks up the bill and refers it to the appropriate House authority—in this case the Committee on Energy and Commerce.

The subcommittee considers the measure. Consultants may be called in, from the Department of Energy or the Department of Transportation, for example. The panel may hold public hearings at which representatives of the oil industry or of federal agencies involved may present their views.

Hearings on important and controversial measures attract intensive news coverage. So do the investigative hearings the congressional committees undertake. These need not stem from consideration of the bill. They can result from a need to look into an issue involving Congress's "watchdog"—or oversight—function, which has been since World War II a powerful and much-used tool.

Action at subcommittee and full committee levels may shape the energy bill for return to the House, which puts it on the proper calendar of business. Or, the bill may die in committee.

A bill put on the calendar usually comes up for debate. Discussion may be routine; committee work by party leaders often governs the bill's fate. Debate also may include oratory ranging from dull to inspired, and orators from little noted to long remembered.

Felix Walker, a legislator of the 1820s, was known as "old oil-jug" because of his many flowing speeches dedicated to Buncombe County in his North Carolina district. Opponents characterized his flowery references to his home district as nonsense, leading to such additions to the language as "bunk" and "debunking."

House rules now limit debate, usually to one hour. Senators are privileged to—and occasionally do—talk around the clock. In both houses, everything said is recorded by official reporters.

UNITED STATES CAPITOL POLICE

GRADUATES *of the United States Capitol Police Recruit Officers Class 160, May 14, 2009, pose on the Capitol's west front grounds.*

UNITED STATES CAPITOL POLICE

BOWED IN PRAYER, *the United States Capitol Police Honor Guard present the colors in a solemn ceremony.*

They work at the bottom dais of the rostrum in the House; in the Senate they move near the speakers to catch every phrase

After a measure is passed by the House, it is sent to the Senate for another round of study, debate, and voting. Differences between the House and Senate may be accepted by the originating body, or they may be worked out in conference committees composed of members from each chamber. Either chamber may originate a bill, with the constitutional exception that all revenue measures begin in the House.

Once approved by the Senate and House, the bill goes to the president, whose signature makes the bill the law of the land. Should the president veto it, the bill can still be enacted by a two-thirds vote of both houses.

From the galleries, visitors see the surface pageantry of this complex process. Moreover, since 1979, the public at large also has had a chance to see a show that has created a new

HOUSE TV CONTROL ROOM
monitors sessions on the floor of the House of Representatives and beams the proceedings via cable television across the nation. Cameras cover House activities, televised since 1979. An operator working the keyboard helps the viewing audience identify a representative on camera by displaying the member's name across the television screen.

cult of Congress-watchers.

In spring of that year, the House authorized the launching of the first live radio and television coverage of proceedings on the House floor. The Senate allowed broadcasting its sessions beginning in June 1986. Today, broadcasts by the Cable-Satellite Public Affairs Network (C-SPAN) give audiences across the nation a first-hand look at the behavior of their elected representatives in action.

In the ordinary procedures of both houses, the workday starts in the respective chambers when the Speaker of the House and the president of the Senate call the sessions to order, usually at 12 noon. Chaplains offer a prayer. Clerks read bills and record votes. Parliamentarians advise on rules and precedent. Members who hold the important posts of majority and minority leaders and whips direct political strategy in carrying out their parties' legislative programs.

Just learning how Congress conducts its business is an undertaking in itself. Freshman legislators, old hands say, need at least a full session merely to grasp the rules and customs they must follow. As Speaker James Beauchamp "Champ" Clark put it, "A new Congressman must begin at the foot of the class and spell up."

When Congress is in session, no offices are busier behind the scenes than each chamber's document room. Through these rooms flow endless streams of bills. Distributing these bills is the daily responsibility of the Capitol's youngest workers, the congressional pages. It is the job of the pages to see that legislators' desks are supplied with the necessary materials including a copy of the *Congressional Record*, as well as to run errands during sessions.

The House began using messengers in 1789. The earliest recorded instance of boys being employed as messengers was during the 20th Congress (1827–29). Daniel Webster is credited with appointing the first Senate page in 1829; he was nine-year-old Grafton Hanson, a descendant of John Hanson, president of the Continental Congress. Today pages are older (they must be juniors in high school), but they still are chosen by the legislators. The first female pages were two sixteen-year-olds appointed by senators Jacob Javits and Charles Percy in 1971. The first female House page was appointed by Speaker Carl Albert in 1973.

UNLIKE PAGES, who work directly for members of Congress, the United States Capitol Police has become a professional rather than a patronage organization. The force, which originated from a single night watchman employed in 1801, now has more than 1,700 members.

Routine duties call for a delicate balance of security and openness. The police officers must protect members, their staffs, and visiting heads of state and other dignitaries and at the same time guard the right of citizens to have access to their elected representatives. With personnel divided into three daily work shifts, the Capitol Police maintain round-the-clock security, seven days a week, for the 47-block complex of congressional buildings.

Occasionally the job can become more than routine. The force has dealt with disturbances ranging from minor incidents to destructive political violence. One dramatic event came in 1954 when four Puerto Rican nationalists opened fire from the gallery into the House Chamber below. Five representatives were wounded.

In 1971, a bomb exploded in a men's room in the old Senate wing. The blast caused extensive damage, but no injuries, probably because it went off about 1:30 a.m. In November 1983, a bomb explosion in a second-floor corridor not far from the Senate Chamber also resulted in considerable damage but, again, no casualties.

Tragically, Capitol Police Officer Jacob Joseph Chestnut and Detective John Michael Gibson lost their lives on July 24, 1998, when a deranged gunman opened fire inside the building's east front entrance. Congress responded with unprecedented honors. The two lay in honor in the Capitol rotunda—Chestnut becoming the first African American accorded that privilege—and a memorial plaque was placed near the entrance they guarded, renamed the Chestnut–Gibson Memorial Door.

Confronted by such threats and by increasing terrorism—brought home by the attacks of September 11, 2001—the Capitol Police maintains units specially trained to respond to terrorist attack, hazardous devices, and barricade or hostage situations.

These events demonstrated that as it entered its third century, the Capitol would need once more to adapt and expand to meet the challenges of changing times.

SUBWAYS *provide a quick passage from Senate and House offices to the Capitol.*

ARCHITECT OF THE CAPITOL

IN THE CAPITOL ROTUNDA, *Congress and official Washington turned out to honor the first woman to members of Congress attended the ceremony for Rosa Parks on October 30, 2005. Parks was also the first non- after Capitol Police Officer Jacob Joseph Chestnut, to be so honored. Congress also approved placing a*

ARCHITECT OF THE CAPITOL

*lie in honor in the Capitol rotunda. The president and
government official and only the second African American,
statue of Parks in the Capitol's National Statuary Hall.*

131

Capitol Visitor Center

Charles Moore, chairman of the Commission on Fine Arts, observed at the beginning of the twentieth century that the Capitol's "highest value lies in the fact that it never was, and it never will be, finished." Moore predicted that the Capitol's nineteenth-century evolution as the symbol of American representative government would continue in the twentieth century.

The Capitol complex, indeed, grew larger since the late 1890s. The first office buildings for House and Senate members and their staffs were added in the first decade of the 1900s. The Library of Congress and the Supreme Court, both previously quartered within the Capitol, moved to their own buildings on Capitol Hill in 1897 and 1935, respectively.

Changing standards of historic preservation affected the Capitol's physical appearance since the late 1950s. The east front extension of 1958–62 that replicated the historic sandstone facade in marble was followed in the 1980s by the restoration of the original sandstone west front.

Likewise, the Old Senate and Old Supreme Court chambers were restored as historical showpieces in the 1970s, conservation to clean and restore Brumidi's artwork commenced, and the Statue of Freedom was brought down by helicopter for repair and restoration in 1993.

Evolving attitudes toward history and the need for the Capitol to reflect the nation's diversity led to more inclusive memorials and artwork. Tributes to women, Native Americans, and African Americans helped make the Capitol more representative of the nation.

Tributes to African Americans included the bronze bust of Martin Luther King, Jr., by sculptor John Wilson (see p. 100) unveiled in the Capitol rotunda in 1986. The inspirational civil rights leader became the first African American honored with a bust in the United States Capitol. The portrait by artist Simmie Knox of the first African American senator to serve a full term, Blanche Kelso Bruce of Mississippi, was placed in the Senate wing in 2002.

The House placed a portrait by Kadir Nelson of the first African American woman elected to Congress, Shirley Chisholm of New York, in 2009. Rosa Parks, the civil rights pioneer of the 1955 Montgomery bus boycott, lay in honor in the rotunda (*see pp. 130–131*) following her death in 2005. Congress also passed legislation directing that a statue of Parks be placed in National Statuary Hall.

SECURITY BECAME the overriding concern as Congress prepared for its third century in the Capitol. Security—not only for legislators and their staffs, but also for the millions of visitors who come to witness free representative government in action—provided the context for the creation of the U. S. Capitol Visitor Center (CVC).

The idea of a visitor center originated in the mid-1970s when then-Architect of the Capitol George M. White sought to create a master plan for the Capitol's future development. However, funding lagged until the shooting deaths of two Capitol Police officers prompted Congress to authorize funds in 1999.

THE STATUE OF FREEDOM, *painstakingly repaired and restored to its original patina, waits on the east plaza to be hoisted by helicopter back to the top of the dome in 1993. Lightning rod tips project from the bronze statue's eagle-feathered headdress.*

ARCHITECT OF THE CAPITOL

"This project is one of historic dimensions," wrote Alan Hantman, the architect of the Capitol in 1999. "It constitutes the last possibility to extend the Capitol within the historic framework of the grounds."

Excavation began in August 2002 and the center opened in December 2008. Providing 580,000 square feet of space on three levels below the east front plaza, the CVC is nearly three-quarters the size of the historic Capitol.

The CVC provides much-needed visitor amenities, including educational exhibits, restrooms, and a restaurant. "We've been waiting for this for years," said one appreciative tourist.

Entering down sloping tulip-poplar-lined walkways, visitors pass through screening checkpoints that eliminate the previous long lines.

The millions of tourists who visit each year proceed through Emancipation Hall, the 20,000 square foot space graced by the restored original plaster model of Thomas Crawford's Statue of Freedom. Two huge 30- by 70-foot skylights provide dramatic views of the Capitol dome.

Emancipation Hall honors the contribution of enslaved African Americans in the construction of the United States Capitol and the long struggle against slavery.

Representative Zach Wamp of Tennessee, who introduced the bill to name the hall, observed, "What we name important places and spaces says a lot about who we are and what we have learned. This will be the largest room in the Capitol and will ensure that future generations of Americans will think about the process of freedom."

Statues from the National Statuary Hall collection were placed in Emancipation Hall and other areas of the CVC, helping to relieve the overcrowding in the Capitol. The twenty-four statues in the CVC reflect the nation's diversity. Six depict women—Mother Joseph, Jeannette Rankin, Sakakawea, Maria L. Sanford, Sarah Winnemucca, and Helen Keller.

The bronze statue of Keller was unveiled in the rotunda on October 7, 2009. The world-renowned activist for the disabled is depicted as a seven-year-old child at a water pump at her home in Tuscumbia, Alabama, where, blind and deaf since infancy, she first learned to sign the word "water."

Also among the 24 statues are five of Native Americans—Sakakawea, Winnemucca, Po'Pay, Chief Washakie, and Pacific Island native King Kamehameha I of Hawaii. Organizer of the Pueblo Revolt against the Spanish colonizers

ARCHITECT OF THE CAPITOL

CAPITOL VISITOR CENTER'S EMANCIPATION HALL *is the scene for the unveiling of the bust of abolitionist and women's rights leader Sojourner Truth on April 28, 2009, by Speaker of the House Nancy Pelosi and First Lady Michelle Obama, seen in the lower right. Thomas Crawford's original plaster model of the Statue of Freedom forms a dramatic backdrop for the ceremony.*

VISITORS *enter the Capitol Visitor Center on opening day, December 2, 2008, the 145th anniversary of the installation of the final section of the Statue of Freedom on top of the dome.*

ARCHITECT OF THE CAPITOL

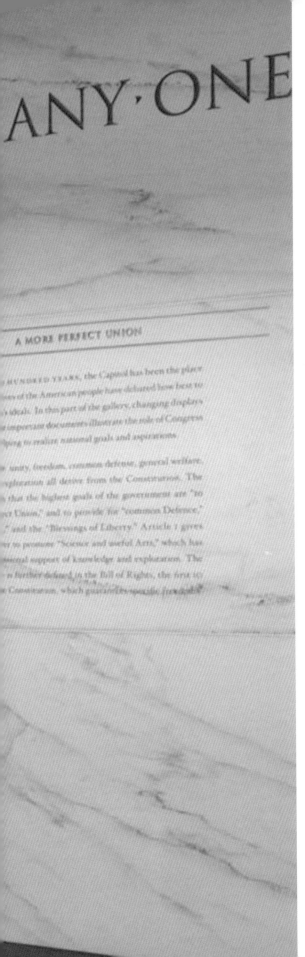

CENTERPIECE OF EXHIBITION HALL *is this 11-foot high touchable model of the Capitol dome. Lighting of the model simulates a day/night cycle. The back of the model is cut away to depict the dome's inner and outer cast-iron construction and the interior of the rotunda including its artistic decoration.*

of what is now New Mexico, Po'Pay is shown holding a bear fetish and the knotted rope used to coordinate the timing of the uprising. The statue of Wyoming's Chief Washakie, the Shoshone warrior and spokesman, is bronze with details painted on the clothing in color.

Passing through Emancipation Hall, visitors enter the 16,500 square-foot Exhibition Hall. Here they find original documents and artifacts (including the Lincoln catafalque), an 11-foot touchable model of the Capitol dome, and interactive stations and two small theaters with films and live television feeds from the House and Senate when in session.

Two 93-foot-long curving marble walls display original historic documents that highlight the efforts of Congress to move the nation toward "a more perfect Union." Documents loaned by the House and Senate, the Library of Congress, and the Office of the Architect of the Capitol are changed periodically to keep the exhibit fresh. Among the documents visitors might see are President John F. Kennedy's speech to Congress vowing to put a man on the moon, Thomas Jefferson's confidential letter to Congress asking for funds for the Lewis and Clark Expedition, and Congressman Abraham Lincoln's 1849 draft bill seeking to emancipate slaves in the District of Columbia.

(Continued on page 140)

ARCHITECT OF THE CAPITOL

ARCHITECT OF THE CAPITOL

HOUSE THEATER *is one of two small theaters located in Exhibition Hall that feature short films on the histories of the House of Representatives and the Senate. Live video feeds from each chamber are seen when Congress is in session. The national motto, "In God We Trust," inscribed above the screen, also appears behind the Speaker's rostrum in the House of Representatives Chamber.*

ALCOVES *housing artifacts, documents, images, and videos in Exhibition Hall tell the multifaceted history of Congress and the Capitol. Detailed architectural models in low-level cases permit viewers to trace the physical growth of Capitol Hill from a rural landscape to its current complex of buildings.*

ARCHITECT OF THE CAPITOL

ARCHITECT OF THE CAPITOL

COMFORTABLE SEATING *awaits visitors in one of two orientation theaters in the spacious CVC. Here viewers see a short film, "Out of Many, One." Highlighting the establishment of the nation's representative form of government, the history of Congress, and the evolution of the Capitol, the film prepares visitors to tour the building's historic spaces.*

ARCHITECT OF THE CAPITOL

ALAN M. HANTMAN, FAIA,
became tenth architect of the Capitol in 1997. During his ten-year tenure, he supervised construction of the Capitol Visitor Center, renovation of the U.S. Botanic Garden Conservatory, rehabilitation of the Capitol dome, and conservation of the Brumidi Corridors. He also helped develop new security measures.

ARCHITECT OF THE CAPITOL

STEPHEN T. AYERS, AIA, LEED AP,
became acting architect of the Capitol following Alan Hantman's retirement in 2007. In May 2010, the Senate confirmed Ayers's appointment as architect of the Capitol. Responsible for the operation of the Capitol complex, Ayers has brought an emphasis on sustainable practices to the organization.

Before moving on to tour the Capitol, visitors go to one of two orientation theaters to view a film introduction to the Capitol and Congress. Those who have passes for guided Capitol tours—available through congressional offices, the Capitol Visitor Services online reservation system, and at information decks in Emancipation Hall—then take escalators up into the historic Capitol.

Situated on the west side of Exhibition Hall is the bust of Sojourner Truth. Unveiled in 2009, it is the first sculpture in the Capitol honoring an African American woman.

Born into slavery in New York as Isabella Baumfree in 1797, she named herself Sojourner Truth in 1843. Preaching abolition and women's rights throughout the North before the Civil War, Truth won fame for her extemporaneous speech to the Ohio Women's Rights Convention in 1851, later published under the title "Ain't I a Woman?" During the Civil War, Truth recruited black troops for the Union Army and met with President Lincoln seeking to improve conditions for African Americans.

Also featured is the bust of Raoul Wallenberg, the Swedish diplomat credited with saving the lives of tens of thousands of Jews during World War II.

Beyond the many statues, exhibits, and other amenities, the CVC also contains offices and meeting rooms for members of Congress and support services. Among these spaces are the two-story Congressional Auditorium, state-of-the-art technical support facilities, and access tunnels.

The largest addition to the Capitol in its more than 200-year history, the CVC was designed and built to endure. As Hantman stated, "The

ARCHITECT OF THE CAPITOL

NEW MAIN VISITOR ENTRANCE
*to the Capitol, the Capitol Visitor Center
provides a never-before-seen view of the
Capitol from 18 feet below street level. The
center's mission is "to provide a welcoming
and educational environment for visitors
. . . resulting in a seamless, positive visitor
experience . . . comprised of highly personal moments that will inform, involve
and inspire those who come to see the
U. S. Capitol."*

*By combining security and comfortable
amenities with modern educational tech-
nology, the CVC makes the Capitol more
accessible, convenient, secure, and informa-
tive. One million visitors passed through the
center during its first five months.*

visitor center must be designed in a manner
worthy of that universal symbol of representative democracy."

On the CVC's stone walls are the words
of the document that continues to define this
nation's experiment in representative government—the Constitution of the United States—
and its Preamble's immortal opening words:
"We the People."

AS VISITORS peruse CVC exhibits, view
the orientation film, and tour the Capitol,
they are reminded that the Capitol has been a
living stage for national events ever since its
first small wing was occupied in November
1800. Its drama-filled past is one of the reasons
that visitors find the building so fascinating,
and that novelists, playwrights, and filmmakers
take real-life plots from its history. The Capitol
has been and will continue to be "a place of
resounding deeds."

From its burning by the British in the War
of 1812, through the trauma of the Civil War,
two world wars and the Cold War, the periodic
scourge of devastating economic woes, and the
threat of international terrorism, the lawmakers'
home has remained an integral force in the making of a federal metropolis and the rise of a great
world power.

In the midst of the Civil War, President
Lincoln sent an address to Congress pleading for
action to save the Union as "the last best hope of
earth." "Fellow citizens," he wrote, "we cannot
escape history." No one who visits the Capitol
can escape its history, ideals, and the promise
of representative government, for here it is that
"We the People" govern.

Index

Boldface indicates illustrations;
italic refers to picture legends (captions)

The Endpapers

*W*HAT *the Declaration of Independence had proclaimed—the heady concept of man's "unalienable" right to "life, liberty, and the pursuit of happiness"—the Constitution forged into reality. Independence had been won, and the government that followed had proved a rope of sand, when delegates from the floundering states met in Philadelphia's Independence Hall on May 25, 1787.*

Remarkable men all—Jefferson called them an "assembly of demigods"—they convened to amend weaknesses of the Articles of Confederation that bound the nation. But daringly they launched a new government, working behind guarded doors, the cobbled streets outside earth-covered to muffle traffic noise. On September 17 their work was done: a document destined to "...secure the blessings of liberty to ourselves and our posterity...."

(front endpaper).

*B*UT *first an infant Congress—to meet criticisms that the Constitution lacked clear-cut guarantees of freedom of speech, religion, and other vital rights—drafted 12 amendments. Ten were ratified by the states and became known as the Bill of Rights (back endpaper).*

The National Archives in Washington, D.C., safeguards America's treasures: the Declaration, the Constitution, and the Bill of Rights. Voices drop to whispers when the documents are displayed in cases designed to protect the priceless contents from harmful effects of air and light.